The
Supporters'
Guide
to
Northern Irish
Football
2006

EDITOR
John Robinson

Third Edition

For details of our range of around 1,200 books and hundreds of DVDs and videos, visit our web site or contact us using the information shown below.

British Library Cataloguing in Publication Data
A catalogue record for this book is available from the British Library

ISBN 1-86223-130-3

Printed by The Cromwell Press

FOREWORD

We wish to thank the club secretaries and officials, particularly Aidan Murphy and Jim Gallagher, for their assistance in providing the information in this guide and yearbook. In addition, we thank Marshall Gillespie for providing the statistical information for the 2004/2005 season and David McVeigh of the Irish F.A. for allowing us to include the 2005/2006 season's fixtures. Our thanks also go to Bob Budd for the cover artwork and Michael Robinson for page layouts.

At the time of going to press, Coleraine FC were on the brink of bankruptcy but we have, nevertheless, included them this time in the hope that the club will survive.

Additional copies of this guide can be obtained directly from us at the address shown on the facing page or, alternatively, via our web site –

www.supportersguides.com

Finally, we would like to wish our readers a happy and safe spectating season.

John Robinson
EDITOR

CONTENTS

Irish Premier League

Address
20 Windsor Avenue, Belfast   BT9 7FB

Phone
(028) 9066-9458

Fax
(028) 9066-7620

Web site
www.irishpremierleague.com

Clubs for the 2005/2006 Season

ARDS FC

Founded: 1902
Former Names: Ards United FC
Nickname: 'The Red & Blues'
Ground: Clandeboye Park, Bangor, Co. Down
Record Attendance: 6,000
Pitch Size: 105 × 65 yards

Colours: Red and Blue striped shirts with Blue shorts
Telephone Nº: (028) 9182-8328
Ground Capacity: 5,000
Seating Capacity: 500
Web Site: www.ardsfc.co.uk
Correspondence: c/o 20 Hillside Mountain Road, Newtownards   BT23 4UR

GENERAL INFORMATION

Car Parking: At the ground
Coach Parking: At the ground
Nearest Railway Station: Bangor
Nearest Bus Station: Bangor
Club Shop: None
Opening Times: –
Telephone Nº: –

ADMISSION INFO (2005/2006 PRICES)

Adult Standing: £6.00
Adult Seating: £7.00
Senior Citizen/Junior Standing: £3.00
Senior Citizen/Junior Seating: £4.00
Programme Price: £1.50

DISABLED INFORMATION

Wheelchairs: Accommodated
Helpers: Admitted
Prices: Normal prices apply
Disabled Toilets: Available in the Social Club
Contact: (028) 9182-8328   (Bookings are not necessary)

Travelling Supporters' Information:
Routes: Take the A2 to Bangor and just before the Town Centre, turn right at the traffic lights directly after the railway bridge. Continue past the church and turn right into Clandeboye Road. The ground is situated on the right after ¼ mile.

ARMAGH CITY FC

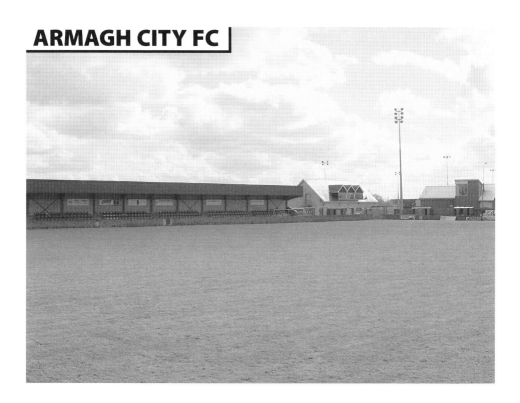

Founded: 1964
Former Names: Milford Everton FC
Nickname: 'Eagles'
Ground: Holm Park, Ardmore, Newry Road, Armagh   BT60 1JD
Record Attendance: 1,750
Pitch Size: 112 × 70 yards

Colours: Azure Blue shirts with Black shorts
Telephone Nº: (028) 3751-1560
Ground Capacity: 2,800
Seating Capacity: 330
Web Site: www.armaghcityfc.com

GENERAL INFORMATION
Car Parking: At the ground
Coach Parking: At the ground
Nearest Railway Station: Portadown (11 miles)
Nearest Bus Station: Armagh (1½ miles)
Club Shop: None
Opening Times: –
Telephone Nº: –

ADMISSION INFO (2005/2006 PRICES)
Adult Standing: £6.00
Adult Seating: £7.00
Senior Citizen/Junior Standing: £4.00
Senior Citizen/Junior Seating: £5.00
Note: One Junior is admitted free with each paying adult
Programme Price: £1.50

DISABLED INFORMATION
Wheelchairs: Accommodated to the front of the Main Stand
Helpers: Admitted
Prices: Normal prices apply for the disabled and helpers
Disabled Toilets: Available adjacent to the disabled area
Contact: (028) 3751-1560   (Bookings are necessary)

Travelling Supporters' Information:
Routes: Follow any route to the City of Armagh. At the junction of the A3 and A28 in Armagh city centre, take the A3 following signs for Newry, pass the Police Station on the right and continue uphill for about a mile. After travelling down hill, turn left into the road signposted for the Ardmore Complex, take the first right then continue for ½ mile. The ground is situated at the end of this road on the left hand side.   Alternatively, if you are travelling along the A3 from the direction of Newry, turn right at the city boundary (30mph speed limit) into the road signposted for the Ardmore Complex, then as above.

BALLYMENA UNITED FC

Founded: 1928
Former Names: None
Nickname: 'The Braidmen'
Ground: The Showgrounds, Warden Street, Ballymena   BT43 7DR
Record Attendance: Not known
Pitch Size: 109 × 70 yards

Colours: Sky Blue shirts with White shorts
Telephone Nº: (028) 2565-2049
Ground Capacity: 3,000
Seating Capacity: 2,000
Web Site: www.bufc.info

GENERAL INFORMATION

Car Parking: At the ground
Coach Parking: At the ground
Nearest Railway Station: Ballymena (1 mile)
Nearest Bus Station: Ballymena
Club Shop: Yes
Opening Times: Matchdays only
Telephone Nº: –

ADMISSION INFO (2005/2006 PRICES)

Adult Standing: £7.00
Adult Seating: £7.00
Senior Citizen/Junior Standing: £3.50
Senior Citizen/Junior Seating: £3.50
Programme Price: £1.50

DISABLED INFORMATION

Wheelchairs: Accommodated
Helpers: Admitted
Prices: Normal prices apply for the disabled and helpers
Disabled Toilets: Available
Contact: (028) 2565-2049   (Bookings are not necessary)

Travelling Supporters' Information:
Routes: Take the A36/A26 into Ballymena and follow the signs for the Showgrounds. In the Town Centre, at the junction of the A42 and A43 by the Fairhill Shopping Centre, turn off at the roundabout into Warden Street. The ground is situated at the end of the road after about ¼ mile.

CLIFTONVILLE FC

Founded: 1879
Former Names: None
Nickname: 'The Reds'
Ground: Solitude, Cliftonville Street, Belfast, BT14 6LP
Record Attendance: 28,600
Pitch Size: 130 × 72 yards

Colours: Red shirts with White shorts
Telephone Nº: (028) 9075-4628
Ground Capacity: 5,000
Seating Capacity: 2,000
Web Site: www.cliftonvillefc.net

GENERAL INFORMATION
Car Parking: Street Parking only
Coach Parking: By police direction
Nearest Railway Station: Belfast
Nearest Bus Station: Belfast
Club Shop: At the ground
Opening Times: Before and after home games. Orders are accepted through the web site
Telephone Nº: (028) 9086-3002

ADMISSION INFO (2005/2006 PRICES)
Adult Standing: £6.00
Adult Seating: £7.00
Senior Citizen/Junior Standing: £3.00
Senior Citizen/Junior Seating: £4.00
Programme Price: £2.00

DISABLED INFORMATION
Wheelchairs: No specific accommodation but admitted
Helpers: Admitted
Prices: Normal prices apply
Disabled Toilets: None
Contact: (028) 9075-4628   (Bookings are necessary)

Travelling Supporters' Information:
Routes: The ground is situated in the North of Belfast in Cliftonville Street. Exit the M2 onto the A12 Ring Road at Junction 1A and turn right into Clifton Street. Bear right into Antrim Road at Carlisle Circus. Turn left at the Church into Cliftonville Road and the ground is situated on the right after about ½ mile.

COLERAINE FC

Founded: 1927
Former Names: Formed by the amalgamation of Coleraine Alexandra FC and Coleraine Olympic FC
Nickname: 'Bannsiders'
Ground: The Showgrounds, Ballycastle Road, Coleraine   BT52 2DY
Record Attendance: 12,500 (vs Spurs in the 1970s)

Pitch Size: 120 × 80 yards
Colours: Blue and White striped shirts, Blue shorts
Telephone Nº: (028) 7035-3655
Ground Capacity: 4,900
Seating Capacity: 1,400
Web Site: www.colerainefc.com

GENERAL INFORMATION

Car Parking: At the ground
Coach Parking: Adjacent to the ground
Nearest Railway Station: Coleraine (¼ mile)
Nearest Bus Station: Coleraine (¼ mile)
Club Shop: At the ground
Opening Times: Matchdays only
Telephone Nº: −

ADMISSION INFO (2005/2006 PRICES)

Adult Standing: £6.00
Adult Seating: £8.00
Senior Citizen/Junior Standing: £3.00
Senior Citizen/Junior Seating: £4.00
Under-14s: £1.00
Programme Price: £1.50

DISABLED INFORMATION

Wheelchairs: Accommodated
Helpers: Admitted
Prices: Reduced prices available for disabled and helpers
Disabled Toilets: Available
Contact: (028) 7035-3655   (Bookings are necessary)

Travelling Supporters' Information:
Routes: Take the A26 to Coleraine and join the Ring Road heading towards Portrush. At the "Ballycastle Road Roundabout" signposts exit the Ring Road and follow signs for the Town Centre. The ground is situated on the left after approximately ½ mile.

DUNGANNON SWIFTS FC

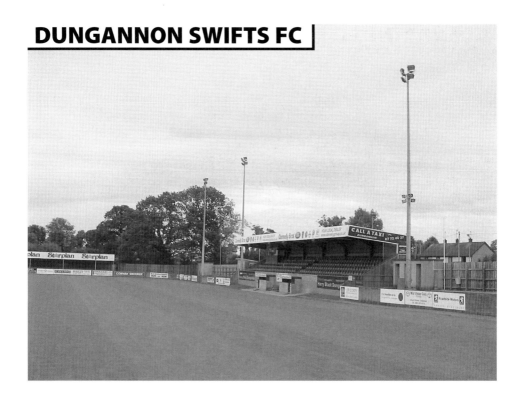

Founded: 1949
Former Names: None
Nickname: 'Swifts'
Ground: Stangmore Park, Dungannon, Co. Tyrone
Record Attendance: 4,876
Pitch Size: 112 × 70 yards

Colours: Royal Blue shirts and shorts
Telephone Nº: (028) 8772-3257
Ground Capacity: 5,000
Seating Capacity: 270
Web Site: www.dungannonswiftsfc.co.uk

GENERAL INFORMATION

Car Parking: At the ground
Coach Parking: At the ground
Nearest Railway Station: Portadown (12 miles)
Nearest Bus Station: Dungannon (1 mile)
Club Shop: In the Clubhouse
Opening Times: Monday to Friday 7.00pm to 11.00pm and Saturdays 11.00am to 11.00pm
Telephone Nº: (028) 8772-3257

ADMISSION INFO (2005/2006 PRICES)

Adult Standing: £6.00
Adult Seating: £7.00
Senior Citizen/Junior Standing: £4.00
Senior Citizen/Junior Seating: £5.00
Programme Price: £1.50

DISABLED INFORMATION

Wheelchairs: Accommodated
Helpers: Admitted
Prices: Normal prices apply for the disabled and helpers
Disabled Toilets: Available
Contact: (028) 8772-3257   (Bookings are not necessary)

Travelling Supporters' Information:
Routes: Take the M1 to Junction 15, then the A29 towards Dungannon. The ground is situated on the outskirts of the town on the right-hand side of the A29 just before the Rugby ground.

GLENAVON FC

Founded: 1889
Former Names: Lurgan Glenavon FC
Nickname: 'Lurgan Blues'
Ground: Mourneview Park, Mourneview Avenue, Lurgan   BT66 8EW
Record Attendance: Not known
Pitch Size: 109 × 76 yards

Colours: Blue shirts with White shorts
Telephone Nº: (028) 3832-2472
Fax Nº: (028) 3832-7694
Ground Capacity: 5,000
Seating Capacity: 3,700
Web Site: www.glenavonfc.com

GENERAL INFORMATION
Car Parking: Street parking
Coach Parking: At the ground
Nearest Railway Station: Lurgan
Nearest Bus Station: Lurgan
Club Shop: At the ground
Opening Times: Matchdays only
Telephone Nº: (028) 3832-2472

ADMISSION INFO (2005/2006 PRICES)
Adult Standing: £8.00
Adult Seating: £8.00
Senior Citizen/Junior Standing: £4.00
Senior Citizen/Junior Seating: £4.00
Under 12s: £1.00
Programme Price: £1.00

DISABLED INFORMATION
Wheelchairs: Accommodated
Helpers: Admitted
Prices: Normal prices apply for the disabled and helpers
Disabled Toilets: Available
Contact: (028) 3832-2472   (Bookings are necessary)

Travelling Supporters' Information:
Routes: Exit the M1 at Junction 10 and take the A26 to Lurgan. Travel to the Queen Street junction and turn left into Malcolm Road. Join Russell Drive, then turn at Lurgan Hospital into Tandragee Road. Turn left at Mourneview Avenue junction and the ground is situated on the left.

GLENTORAN FC

Founded: 1882
Former Names: None
Nickname: 'The Glens'
Ground: The Oval, Parkgate Drive, Belfast, BT4 1EW
Record Attendance: 40,000
Pitch Size: 112 × 70 yards

Colours: Green shirts with White shorts
Telephone Nº: (028) 9045-6137
Fax Nº: (028) 9073-2956
Ground Capacity: 30,000
Seating Capacity: 5,000
Web Site: www.glentoran.net

GENERAL INFORMATION

Car Parking: Street parking only
Coach Parking: At the ground
Nearest Railway Station: Sydenham Hall
Nearest Bus Station: Belfast
Club Shop: At the ground
Opening Times: Matchdays only
Telephone Nº: (028) 9045-7670

ADMISSION INFO (2005/2006 PRICES)

Adult Standing: £8.00
Adult Seating: £8.00
Senior Citizen/Junior Standing: £5.00
Senior Citizen/Junior Seating: £5.00
Programme Price: £1.50

DISABLED INFORMATION

Wheelchairs: Accommodated
Helpers: Admitted
Prices: Normal prices apply for the disabled and helpers
Disabled Toilets: Available
Contact: (028) 9045-7670   (Bookings are not necessary)

Travelling Supporters' Information:
Routes: The Oval is located in East Belfast, on the eastern side of the River Lagan in County Down. From Belfast City Centre: Take the Queen Elizabeth Bridge and travel along the Sydenham Bypass following the directions for the City Airport and Bangor (A2). The Oval is conveniently located off the Bypass. For access to the ground, leave the Bypass at the Harbour Estate (Dee Street), looking out for the giant yellow cranes of the shipyard. The exit and the cranes will be on the left. The Harbour Estate gates are then also on the left but turn right at the mini-roundabout and travel over the road bridge and first left into Mersey Street. The ground is on the left, behind Mersey Street Primary School.

INSTITUTE FC

Founded: 1905
Former Names: None
Nickname: 'Stute'
Ground: Riverside Stadium, YMCA Grounds, 51 Glenshane Road, Drumahoe, Londonderry, BT47 3SF
Record Attendance: Approximately 2,000
Pitch Size: 112 × 72 yards

Colours: Sky Blue shirts with Navy Blue shorts
Telephone Nº: (028) 7130-2129
Ground Capacity: 2,000
Seating Capacity: 600
Web Site: www.institutefc.com

GENERAL INFORMATION
Car Parking: At the ground
Coach Parking: At the ground
Nearest Railway Station: Londonderry (3 miles)
Nearest Bus Station: Londonderry (3 miles)
Club Shop: At the ground
Opening Times: Home matchdays only 1.00pm to 5.00pm
Telephone Nº: (028) 7130-2129

ADMISSION INFO (2005/2006 PRICES)
Adult Standing: £6.00
Adult Seating: £6.00
Senior Citizen/Junior Standing: £4.00
Senior Citizen/Junior Seating: £4.00
Programme Price: £1.50

DISABLED INFORMATION
Wheelchairs: Accommodated
Helpers: Admitted
Prices: Normal prices apply for the disabled and helpers
Disabled Toilets: Available
Contact: (028) 7130-2129   (Bookings are not necessary)

Travelling Supporters' Information:
Routes: From Dublin/Strabane: Take the main road towards Londonderry. On arrival in the city do not cross the Craigavon Bridge, but proceed straight into Waterside following signs for Belfast. Upon passing the hospital, the ground is approximately 1 mile further on the right hand side as you enter the village of Drumahoe; From Londonderry: Cross the Craigavon Bridge and turn left following the signs for Belfast. Then as above; From Belfast/Dungiven: The ground is on the left as you leave Drumahoe.

LARNE FC

Founded: 1890
Former Names: Larne Olympic FC
Nickname: 'The Harbour Rats'
Ground: Inver Park, Inver Road, Larne   BT40 3BW
Record Attendance: Not known
Pitch Size: 110 × 66 yards

Colours: Red shirts with White shorts
Telephone Nº: (028) 7130-2129
Ground Capacity: 6,000
Seating Capacity: 850
Web Site: www.wwwlarnefc.net

GENERAL INFORMATION
Car Parking: At the ground
Coach Parking: At the ground
Nearest Railway Station: Larne
Nearest Bus Station: Larne
Club Shop: At the ground
Opening Times: Matchdays only
Telephone Nº: (028) 7130-2129

ADMISSION INFO (2005/2006 PRICES)
Adult Standing: £7.00
Adult Seating: £8.00
Senior Citizen Standing: £5.00
Senior Citizen Seating: £6.00
Junior Standing/Seating: £2.00 (Season tickets available)
Programme Price: £1.50

DISABLED INFORMATION
Wheelchairs: Accommodated
Helpers: Admitted
Prices: Normal prices apply for the disabled and helpers
Disabled Toilets: None
Contact: (07796) 935808 – Sean McVeigh
(Bookings are not necessary)

Travelling Supporters' Information:
Routes: Take the A2 or the A8 to Larne, then at the large roundabout in the Town Centre, take the Carrickfergus Road and follow signs for 'Inver' for the ground.

LIMAVADY UNITED FC

Founded: 1876
Former Names: Alexander FC, Limavady FC and Limavady Wanderers FC
Nickname: 'United' or 'The Lims'
Ground: The Showgrounds, Rathmore Road, Limavady   BT49 0DF
Record Attendance: Not known

Pitch Size: 115 × 75 yards
Colours: Royal Blue shirts and shorts
Telephone Nº: (028) 7776-4351
Ground Capacity: 5,000
Seating Capacity: 300
Web Site: None at present

GENERAL INFORMATION
Car Parking: At the ground
Coach Parking: At the ground
Nearest Railway Station: Londonderry
Nearest Bus Station: Limavady
Club Shop: None
Opening Times: –
Telephone Nº: –

ADMISSION INFO (2005/2006 PRICES)
Adult Standing: £6.00
Adult Seating: £7.00
Senior Citizen/Junior Standing: £4.00
Senior Citizen/Junior Seating: £5.00
Specials: An Under-16s season ticket costs just £10.00 and Under-11s are admitted free of charge.
Programme Price: £1.00

DISABLED INFORMATION
Wheelchairs: Accommodated
Helpers: Admitted
Prices: Normal prices apply for the disabled and helpers
Disabled Toilets: Available
Contact: (028) 7776-4351   (Bookings are necessary)

Travelling Supporters' Information:
Routes: Take the A37 to Limavady and the ground is situated on the main road, ½ mile from the Town Centre on the east (Coleraine) side of the town.

LINFIELD FC

Founded: 1886
Former Names: None
Nickname: 'The Blues'
Ground: Windsor Park, Donegall Avenue, Belfast, BT12 6LW
Record Attendance: 58,000
Pitch Size: 115 × 75 yards

Colours: Royal Blue shirts with White shorts
Telephone Nº: (028) 9024-4198
Ground Capacity: 20,000
Seating Capacity: 14,000
Web Site: www.linfieldfc.com

GENERAL INFORMATION

Car Parking: At the ground and also street parking
Coach Parking: Boucher Road
Nearest Railway Station: Belfast
Nearest Bus Station: Belfast
Club Shop: At the ground
Opening Times: Weekdays and matchdays from 10.00am to 5.00pm (closed on Wednesdays)
Telephone Nº: (028) 9032-9044

ADMISSION INFO (2005/2006 PRICES)

Adult Seating: £8.00
Senior Citizen/Junior Seating: £5.00
Programme Price: £1.50

DISABLED INFORMATION

Wheelchairs: Accommodated
Helpers: Admitted
Prices: Normal prices apply for the disabled and helpers
Disabled Toilets: Available
Contact: (028) 9024-4198   (Bookings are necessary)

Travelling Supporters' Information:
Routes: Exit the M1 at Junction 1 and follow signs into Donegall Road. Just before the railway bridge, turn right into Donegall Avenue and the ground is on the right after ¼ mile.

LISBURN DISTILLERY FC

Founded: 1879
Former Names: Distillery FC
Nickname: 'Whites'
Ground: New Grosvenor Stadium, Ballyskeagh Road, Lambeg, Lisburn, County Antrim
Record Attendance: Not known
Pitch Size: 110 × 72 yards

Colours: White shirts and shorts
Telephone Nº: (028) 9030-1148
Ground Capacity: 7,000
Seating Capacity: 1,600
Web Site: www.lisburn-distillery.net

GENERAL INFORMATION
Car Parking: At the ground
Coach Parking: At the ground
Nearest Railway Station: Lambeg (1 mile)
Nearest Bus Station: Lisburn
Club Shop: At the ground
Opening Times: Matchdays only
Telephone Nº: (028) 9030-1148

ADMISSION INFO (2005/2006 PRICES)
Adult Standing: £7.00
Adult Seating: £7.00
Senior Citizen/Junior Standing: £3.50
Senior Citizen/Junior Seating: £3.50
Programme Price: £1.50

DISABLED INFORMATION
Wheelchairs: Accommodated
Helpers: Admitted
Prices: Normal prices apply for the disabled and helpers
Disabled Toilets: Available
Contact: (028) 9030-1148 (Bookings are necessary)

Travelling Supporters' Information:
Routes: From Belfast and the East: Exit the M1 at Junction 6 and take the turning into Largeymore Link at the exit road roundabout (do not take the Saintfield Road/A49 turning). Turn right at the lights and remain on the Hillhall Road for approximately 2½ miles. Turn left at Drumbeg Mews on the corner of Drumbeg Road, continue down the road then turn left at the T-junction. Follow this road and the ground is on the right just after the M1 motorway has been crossed; From Lisburn City Centre: Head towards Belfast, pass Wallace Park on the left and continue along the Belfast Road until the traffic lights at McBurnies shop, Harmony Hill. Turn right at these lights, pass underneath the railway line and remain on this road for almost 2 miles. The ground is situated on the left after passing a narrow bridge which is preceded by a left-hand bend.

LOUGHGALL FC

Founded: 1897 (Re-formed in 1967)
Former Names: None
Nickname: 'The Villagers'
Ground: Lakeview Park, Ballygasey Road, Loughgall County Armagh
Record Attendance: 1,650
Pitch Size: 112 × 66 yards

Colours: Royal Blue shirts and shorts
Telephone Nº: (028) 3889-1400
Ground Capacity: 3,000
Seating Capacity: 200
Web Site: www.loughgallfc.org

GENERAL INFORMATION
Car Parking: At the ground
Coach Parking: At the ground
Nearest Railway Station: Portadown (5 miles)
Nearest Bus Station: Portadown (5 miles)
Club Shop: At the ground
Opening Times: Matchdays only
Telephone Nº: (028) 3889-1400

ADMISSION INFO (2005/2006 PRICES)
Adult Standing: £6.00
Adult Seating: £6.00
Senior Citizen/Junior Standing: £4.00
Senior Citizen/Junior Seating: £4.00
Programme Price: £1.50

DISABLED INFORMATION
Wheelchairs: Accommodated
Helpers: Admitted
Prices: Normal prices apply for the disabled and helpers
Disabled Toilets: Available
Contact: (028) 3889-1400 (Bookings are not necessary)

Travelling Supporters' Information:
Routes: Loughgall is situated on the B77 mid-way between Armagh and Portadown (when travelling from the M1, exit at Junction 13 and follow the B131). The ground is situated in the village centre opposite the Police Station.

NEWRY CITY FC

Founded: 1923
Former Names: Newry Town FC
Nickname: None
Ground: The Showgrounds, Greenbank Industrial Estate, Newry, County Down   BT34 2QF
Record Attendance: Appoximately 4,500 (1950s)
Pitch Size: 110 × 75 yards

Colours: Blue and White striped shirts, White shorts
Telephone Nº: (028) 3082-5648
Ground Capacity: 5,000
Seating Capacity: 1,000
Web Site: www.newrytown.co.uk

GENERAL INFORMATION

Car Parking: At the ground
Coach Parking: At the ground
Nearest Railway Station: Newry (2-3 miles)
Nearest Bus Station: Newry (1½ miles)
Club Shop: At the ground
Opening Times: Matchdays only
Telephone Nº: (028) 3082-5648

ADMISSION INFO (2005/2006 PRICES)

Adult Standing: £7.00
Adult Seating: £8.00
Senior Citizen/Junior Standing: £4.00
Senior Citizen/Junior Seating: £5.00
Programme Price: £2.00

DISABLED INFORMATION

Wheelchairs: Accommodated (lift available in the Stand)
Helpers: Admitted
Prices: Free of charge for disabled. Helpers normal prices
Disabled Toilets: Available
Contact: (028) 3025-2580 (Bookings are necessary)

Travelling Supporters' Information:
Routes: Travelling South, take the M1 following signs for Newry/Dublin. Take the exit at Sprucefield for the A1 and follow signs for the A1 Dublin and Newry. Upon reaching Newry head across the roundabout at the bypass and continue into the City Centre. Pass the Mourne Country Hotel and Ardmore Police Station. After ½ mile go straight on at two roundabouts following signposts for the City Centre. Pass the Brass Monkey Bar on the left and stay to the left going past the Bank of Ireland. Stay to the left at the traffic lights following signs for Dublin and Warrenpoint onto the dual carriageway. At the next junction follow signs for Warrenpoint. Exit to the left at the traffic lights and carry on towards Warrenpoint. After ½ mile turn right at the roundabout into the Greenbank Industrial Estate then immediately left and The Showgrounds are on the right after 200 yards.

PORTADOWN FC

Founded: 1924
Former Names: None
Nickname: 'The Ports'
Ground: Shamrock Park, Brownstown Road, Portadown, County Armagh BT62 3PZ
Record Attendance: 16,500 (1962)
Pitch Size: 110 × 65 yards

Colours: Red shirts and shorts
Telephone Nº: (028) 3833-2726
Fax Nº: (028) 3833-2726
Ground Capacity: 15,000
Seating Capacity: 2,700
Web Site: www.portadownfc.co.uk

GENERAL INFORMATION

Car Parking: Spaces for 200 cars available at the ground
Coach Parking: At the ground
Nearest Railway Station: Portadown (1 mile)
Nearest Bus Station: Fair Green, Portadown (½ mile)
Club Shop: At the ground
Opening Times: Weekdays and Matchdays from 9.30am to 12.00pm
Telephone Nº: (028) 3833-2726

ADMISSION INFO (2005/2006 PRICES)

Adult Standing: £6.00
Adult Seating: £8.00
Senior Citizen/Junior Standing: £3.00
Senior Citizen/Junior Seating: £4.00
Programme Price: £1.50

DISABLED INFORMATION

Wheelchairs: Accommodated
Helpers: Admitted
Prices: Free of charge for the disabled and helpers
Disabled Toilets: Available
Contact: Bill Emerson, c/o club (Bookings not necessary)

Travelling Supporters' Information:
Routes: From Belfast: Take the M1 to Junction 11 then take the M12 then the A3 into Portadown Town Centre. Cross the Bann River and continue along the A3 following signs for Armagh through three sets of traffic lights. Follow the A3 ringroad around the back of Clounagh Junior High School and the Brownstown Estate until a large roundabout is reached. The first exit will take you to Shamrock and on matchdays, Away fans par their cars on this road and walk past the traffic lights to the left to reach the ground. Parking is also available turning right at the traffic lights along the Mahon Road (A27); From North Antrim/East Londonderry: Head for Nutts Corner along the A26. At Nutts Corner Roundabout take the road for Craigavon/Moira A26 until it's conclusion at Moira and Junction 9 of the M1. At Junction 9 take the road to Portadown then follow directions as above.

IRISH FOOTBALL LEAGUE FIRST DIVISION

Address
20 Windsor Avenue, Belfast   BT9 7FB

Phone
(028) 9066-9458

Fax
(028) 9066-7620

Web site
www.irishpremierleague.com

Clubs for the 2005/2006 Season

BALLYCLARE COMRADES FC

Founded: 1919
Former Names: None
Nickname: 'The Comrades'
Ground: Dixon Park, Harrier Way, Ballyclare,
BT39 9BB
Record Attendance: Not known
Pitch Size: 110 × 72 yards

Colours: Red shirts with White trim, White shorts
Telephone Nº: (028) 6638-8600
Ground Capacity: 4,000
Seating Capacity: 200
Web Site: www.ballyclarecomrades.co.uk

GENERAL INFORMATION

Car Parking: Street parking
Coach Parking: By Police direction
Nearest Railway Station: Carrickfergus (8 miles)
Nearest Bus Station: Ballyclare
Club Shop: None
Opening Times: –
Telephone Nº: –

ADMISSION INFO (2005/2006 PRICES)

Adult Standing: £4.00
Adult Seating: £4.00
Senior Citizen/Junior Standing: £2.00
Senior Citizen/Junior Seating: £2.00
Programme Price: £1.00

DISABLED INFORMATION

Wheelchairs: Accommodated
Helpers: Admitted
Prices: Normal prices apply for the disabled and helpers
Disabled Toilets: None
Contact: (028) 6638-8600   (Bookings are not necessary)

Travelling Supporters' Information:
Routes: Exit the M2 at Junction 5 and take the A57 to Ballyclare. The ground is located in the Town Centre adjacent to the supermarket and is easy to find.

BALLYMONEY UNITED FC

Founded: 1944
Former Names: Coronation Blues FC, Ballymoney Athletic FC
Nickname: 'United' or 'The Toon'
Ground: The Showgrounds, North Road, Ballymoney, County Antrim
Record Attendance: 300

Pitch Size: 110 × 72 yards
Colours: White shirts with Black shorts
Telephone Nº: (028) 2766-5831
Ground Capacity: 5,000
Seating Capacity: 100
Web Site: www.ballymoneyunited.co.uk

GENERAL INFORMATION
Car Parking: At the ground
Coach Parking: At the ground
Nearest Railway Station: Ballymoney (¼ mile)
Nearest Bus Station: At Ballymoney Railway Station
Club Shop: 35 Castle Street, Ballymoney
Opening Times: Opens for a short time at 7.30pm on Thursdays, 4.00pm on Fridays, 1.30pm on Saturdays and 12.30pm on Sundays
Telephone Nº: (028) 2766-6054

ADMISSION INFO (2005/2006 PRICES)
Adult Standing/Seating: £4.00
Senior Citizen Standing/Seating: £2.00
Under-16s Standing/Seating: Free of charge
Programme Price: £1.00 (not printed for every game)

DISABLED INFORMATION
Wheelchairs: Accommodated
Helpers: Admitted
Prices: Normal prices apply for the disabled and helpers
Disabled Toilets: Available
Contact: (028) 2765-5446 (Bookings are necessary)

Travelling Supporters' Information:
Routes: Take the B66 into the Town Centre and turn left at the roundabout into North Road. The ground is situated on the left at the end of the road (adjacent to the shopping centre).

BANBRIDGE TOWN FC

Founded: 1947
Former Names: None
Nickname: 'Town'
Ground: Crystal Park, Laws Lane, Castlewellan Road, Banbridge, County Down
Record Attendance: Not known
Pitch Size: 112 × 72 yards

Colours: Red and Black striped shirts, Black shorts
Telephone Nº: (028) 4062-2081 (Clubhouse); (028) 4062-6492 (Club Secretary)
Ground Capacity: 1,500
Seating Capacity: None
Web Site: www.banbridgetownfc.com

GENERAL INFORMATION
Car Parking: Street parking only
Coach Parking: Street parking only
Nearest Railway Station: Portadown (10 miles)
Nearest Bus Station: Banbridge
Club Shop: None
Opening Times: –
Telephone Nº: –

ADMISSION INFO (2005/2006 PRICES)
Adult Standing: £5.00
Adult Seating: £5.00
Senior Citizen/Junior Standing: £2.50
Senior Citizen/Junior Seating: £2.50
Programme Price: Free of charge

DISABLED INFORMATION
Wheelchairs: Accommodated
Helpers: Admitted
Prices: Normal prices apply for the disabled and helpers
Disabled Toilets: None at present but construction is due to begin during the 2005/2006 season
Contact: – (Bookings are not necessary)

Travelling Supporters' Information:
Routes: Exit the A1 on to the A50 for Banbridge. Continue into the Town Centre, turning left into Castlewellan Road, pass the Police Station then turn left just before the Crown buildings. The ground is immediately on the left.

BANGOR FC

Founded: 1918
Former Names: None
Nickname: 'The Seasiders'
Ground: Clandeboye Park, Clandeboye Road, Bangor BT20 3JT
Record Attendance: 6,000
Pitch Size: 105 × 65 yards

Colours: Gold shirts with Royal Blue shorts
Telephone Nº: (028) 9145-7712
Ground Capacity: 5,000
Seating Capacity: 500
Web Site: www.bangorfc.com

GENERAL INFORMATION

Car Parking: At the ground
Coach Parking: At the ground
Nearest Railway Station: Bangor (1 mile)
Nearest Bus Station: Bangor
Club Shop: At the ground
Opening Times: Matchdays only
Telephone Nº: (028) 9145-7712

ADMISSION INFO (2005/2006 PRICES)

Adult Standing: £4.00
Adult Seating: £5.00
Senior Citizen/Junior Standing: £3.00
Senior Citizen/Junior Seating: £4.00
Programme Price: £1.00

DISABLED INFORMATION

Wheelchairs: Accommodated
Helpers: Admitted
Prices: Normal prices apply for the disabled and helpers
Disabled Toilets: Available in the Social Club
Contact: (028) 91-46-9826   (Bookings are not necessary)

Travelling Supporters' Information:
Routes: Approaching Bangor on the main road from Belfast, you will see a flyover. Before you reach the bridge, take the slip road off to the left and follow the signposts for Donaghdee. At the flyover traffic lights, stay in the left hand lane as you turn right over the bridge. Continue until you reach another set of traffic lights with Jollye's pet store on the left. Turn left at these lights into Clandeboye Road and the ground will come into view at the bottom of the hill.

CARRICK RANGERS FC

Founded: 1939
Former Names: None
Nickname: 'Rangers'
Ground: Taylors Avenue, Carrickfergus   BT38 7HF
Record Attendance: Not known
Pitch Size: 105 × 68 yards

Colours: Amber shirts with Black shorts
Telephone Nº: (028) 9332-6396
Club Secretary Telephone Nº: (07921) 670787
Ground Capacity: 5,000
Seating Capacity: 750
Web Site: www.carrickrangers.co.uk

GENERAL INFORMATION

Car Parking: At the ground
Coach Parking: At the ground
Nearest Railway Station: Carrickfergus
Nearest Bus Station: Carrickfergus
Club Shop: At the ground
Opening Times: Matchdays only
Telephone Nº: (028) 9332-6396

ADMISSION INFO (2005/2006 PRICES)

Adult Standing: £5.00
Adult Seating: £5.00
Senior Citizen/Junior Standing: £3.00
Senior Citizen/Junior Seating: £3.00
Programme Price: None

DISABLED INFORMATION

Wheelchairs: Accommodated
Helpers: Admitted
Prices: Normal prices apply for the disabled and helpers
Disabled Toilets: Available
Contact: (028) 9332-6396   (Bookings are not necessary)

Travelling Supporters' Information:
Routes: Take the A2 to Carrickfergus and the ground is situated just off the sea front in Taylors Avenue.

COAGH UNITED FC

Photo courtesy of Normal Bell, Cookstown

Founded: 1970
Former Names: Coagh Swifts FC
Nickname: 'United'
Ground: Hagan Park, 11 Ballinderrybridge Road, Coagh, County Tyrone
Record Attendance: 700
Pitch Size: 110 × 65 yards

Colours: Blue and White shirts with Blue shorts
Telephone Nº: (028) 8673-6073
Ground Capacity: 2,000
Seating Capacity: 100
Web Site: www.coaghunitedfc.co.uk

GENERAL INFORMATION
Car Parking: At the ground and at Coagh Sports Centre
Coach Parking: At the ground and at Coach Sports Centre
Nearest Railway Station: Portadown (30 miles)
Nearest Bus Station: Cookstown – Services available Weekdays 9.30am to 4.00pm – Phone (028) 8676-6440
Club Shop: At the Social Club on Matchdays
Opening Times: Social Club is open Thursdays and Fridays 7.30pm to 11.00pm and on Saturdays 1.00pm to 11.30pm
Telephone Nº: (028) 8673-6073

ADMISSION INFO (2005/2006 PRICES)
Adult Standing/Seating: 4.00
Senior Citizen/Junior Standing/Seating: £2.00
Programme Price: £1.00 (not available for all matches)

DISABLED INFORMATION
Wheelchairs: Accommodated
Helpers: Admitted
Prices: Free for the disabled and normal prices for helpers
Disabled Toilets: Available in the Club House
Contact: (028) 8673-7477 or 8676-2193 (Bookings helpful)

Travelling Supporters' Information:
Routes: The ground is in the centre of Coagh, just off the B160 from Ballyronan.

CRUSADERS FC

Founded: 1898
Former Names: None
Nickname: 'Hatchetmen' or 'The Crues'
Ground: Seaview, Shore Road, Belfast   BT15 3PL
Record Attendance: 11,000
Pitch Size: 108 × 72 yards

Colours: Red and Black striped shirts, Black shorts
Telephone Nº: (028) 9037-0777
Fax Number: (028) 9077-1049
Ground Capacity: 9,000
Seating Capacity: 1,000
Web Site: www.crusadersfc.com

GENERAL INFORMATION

Car Parking: Street parking only
Coach Parking: At the ground
Nearest Railway Station: Belfast
Nearest Bus Station: Belfast
Club Shop: At the ground
Opening Times: Matchdays only
Telephone Nº: (028) 9037-0777 or (07742) 894067

ADMISSION INFO (2005/2006 PRICES)

Adult Standing: £6.00
Adult Seating: £7.00
Senior Citizen/Junior Standing: £4.00
Senior Citizen/Junior Seating: £5.00
Programme Price: £1.50

DISABLED INFORMATION

Wheelchairs: Accommodated
Helpers: Admitted
Prices: Normal prices apply for the disabled and helpers
Disabled Toilets: Available
Contact: (028) 9037-0777   (Bookings are not necessary)

Travelling Supporters' Information:
Routes: Exit the M2 at Junction 1 and take the Shore Road southwards. The ground is on the left after ¼ mile.

DONEGAL CELTIC FC

Founded: 1970
Former Names: None
Nickname: 'The Hoops'
Ground: 32 Suffolk Road, Belfast,   BT11
Record Attendance: Not known
Pitch Size: 110 × 70 yards

Colours: Green & White hooped shirts, White shorts
Telephone N°: (028) 9062-9810
Ground Capacity: 1,500
Seating Capacity: None
Web Site: None

GENERAL INFORMATION
Car Parking: At the ground
Coach Parking: At the ground
Nearest Railway Station: Finaghy
Nearest Bus Station: Belfast City Centre
Club Shop: None
Opening Times: –
Telephone N°: –

ADMISSION INFO (2005/2006 PRICES)
Adult Standing: £3.00
Senior Citizen/Junior Standing: £1.50
Programme Price: £1.00

DISABLED INFORMATION
Wheelchairs: Accommodated
Helpers: Admitted
Prices: Normal prices apply for the disabled and helpers
Disabled Toilets: Available
Contact: (028) 9062-9810   (Bookings are necessary)

Travelling Supporters' Information:
Routes: The ground is situated between Stewartstown Road and Glen Road to the west of Belfast.

DUNDELA FC

Founded: 1895
Former Names: None
Nickname: 'The Duns'
Ground: Wilgar Park, Wilgar Street, Strandtown, Belfast   BT4 3BL
Record Attendance: Not known
Pitch Size: 100 × 65 yards

Colours: Green and White shirts with White shorts
Telephone Nº: (028) 9065-3109
Ground Capacity: 3,000
Seating Capacity: 40
Web Site: www.dundelafc.co.uk

GENERAL INFORMATION
Car Parking: At the ground
Coach Parking: At the ground
Nearest Railway Station: Belfast
Nearest Bus Station: Belfast
Club Shop: None
Opening Times: –
Telephone Nº: –

ADMISSION INFO (2005/2006 PRICES)
Adult Standing: £4.00
Adult Seating: £4.00
Senior Citizen/Junior Standing: £1.00
Senior Citizen/Junior Seating: £1.00
Programme Price: No programmes produced

DISABLED INFORMATION
Wheelchairs: Accommodated
Helpers: Admitted
Prices: Normal prices apply for the disabled and helpers
Disabled Toilets: Available in the Social Club
Contact: (028) 9065-3109   (Bookings are necessary)

Travelling Supporters' Information:
Routes: Exit the M3 at the junction with the A2 and follow signs for the A20 into Newtownards Road. Turn left at the main junction into Holywood Road. Pass the Police Station and turn right into Dundela Avenue. The ground is on the left at the junction with Dundela Crescent.

HARLAND & WOLFF WELDERS FC

Founded: 1965
Former Names: None
Nickname: 'The Welders'
Ground: Tillysburn Park, Holywood Road, Belfast, BT4
Record Attendance: 700
Pitch Size: 110 × 66 yards

Colours: Yellow shirts with Black shorts
Telephone Nº: (028) 9076-1214
Ground Capacity: 1,500
Seating Capacity: None
Web Site: None
E-mail: welders@btinternet.com

GENERAL INFORMATION
Car Parking: At the ground
Coach Parking: At the ground
Nearest Railway Station: Central Station (2 miles)
Nearest Bus Station: Belfast
Club Shop: None
Opening Times: –
Telephone Nº: –

ADMISSION INFO (2005/2006 PRICES)
Adult Standing: £4.00
Senior Citizen/Junior Standing: £1.00
Programme Price: None

DISABLED INFORMATION
Wheelchairs: Accommodated
Helpers: Admitted
Prices: Normal prices apply
Disabled Toilets: None
Contact: (028) 9076-1214 (Bookings are not necessary)

Travelling Supporters' Information:
Routes: Tillysburn Park is situated next to the airport. Take the A2 bypass to the junction with the A504 (Holywood Road) and the ground is on the right hand side next to the aircraft park.

MOYOLA PARK FC

Founded: 1880
Former Names: None
Nickname: 'The Park'
Ground: Moyola Park, Bridge Street, Castledawson, County Londonderry
Record Attendance: 2,800
Pitch Size: 110 × 65 yards

Colours: Royal Blue shirts and shorts
Telephone Nº: (028) 7946-8745
Ground Capacity: 2,000
Seating Capacity: None
Web Site: www.moyolaparkfc.co.uk
Contact Address: R. Loughrey, 7 Bridge Street, Castledawson BT45 8AD
Contact Telephone Nº: (028) 7946-8728

GENERAL INFORMATION
Car Parking: At the ground
Coach Parking: Bridge Street
Nearest Railway Station: Antrim (15 miles)
Nearest Bus Station: Magherafelt (3 miles)
Club Shop: At the Social Club
Social Club: 16 Main Street, Castledawson

ADMISSION INFO (2005/2006 PRICES)
Adult Standing: £5.00
Senior Citizen Standing: £2.00
Junior Standing: Free of charge
Programme Price: £1.00

DISABLED INFORMATION
Wheelchairs: Accommodated
Helpers: Admitted
Prices: Normal prices apply for the disabled and helpers
Disabled Toilets: Available
Contact: (028) 7946-8728 (Bookings are not necessary)

Travelling Supporters' Information:
Routes: Castledawson is situated 1 mile to the North-East of the A6 on the A54. The ground is located in Bridge Street down a lane beside the church.

TOBERMORE UNITED FC

Founded: 1965
Former Names: None
Nickname: 'United'
Ground: Fortwilliam Park, Maghera Road, Tobermore
Record Attendance: 2,500
Pitch Size: 112 × 73 yards

Colours: Red and Black striped shirts, Black shorts
Telephone N°: (028) 7964-5959
Ground Capacity: 2,500
Seating Capacity: None
Web Site: www.mabus-arts.com/tufc/

GENERAL INFORMATION
Car Parking: At the ground
Coach Parking: At the ground
Nearest Railway Station: Antrim (20 miles)
Nearest Bus Station: Magherafelt
Club Shop: None
Opening Times: –
Telephone N°: –

ADMISSION INFO (2005/2006 PRICES)
Adult Standing: £4.00
Senior Citizen/Junior Standing: £2.00
Programme Price: None

DISABLED INFORMATION
Wheelchairs: Accommodated
Helpers: Admitted
Prices: Normal prices apply for the disabled and helpers
Disabled Toilets: Available
Contact: (028) 7964-2425   (Bookings are not necessary)

Travelling Supporters' Information:
Routes: Tobermore is located to the south of the A6 on the A29. The ground itself is situated ½ mile to the north of the village on the left-hand side of the road.

IRISH FOOTBALL LEAGUE SECOND DIVISION

Address
20 Windsor Avenue, Belfast   BT9 7FB

Phone
(028) 9066-9458

Fax
(028) 9066-7620

Web site
www.irishpremierleague.com

Clubs for the 2005/2006 Season

ANNAGH UNITED FC

Founded: 1963
Former Names: None
Nickname: None
Ground: Tandragee Road, Portadown, Co. Armagh
Record Attendance: 500
Pitch Size: 110 × 71 yards

Colours: Red and Black shirts with Black shorts
Telephone Nº: None
Ground Capacity: 1,500
Seating Capacity: 120
Web Site: None

GENERAL INFORMATION
Car Parking: At the ground
Coach Parking: At the ground
Nearest Railway Station: Portadown
Nearest Bus Station: Craigavon
Club Shop: None
Opening Times: –
Telephone Nº: –

ADMISSION INFO (2005/2006 PRICES)
Adult Standing: £3.00
Adult Seating: £4.00
Senior Citizen/Junior Standing: £2.00
Senior Citizen/Junior Seating: £2.00
Programme Price: None

DISABLED INFORMATION
Wheelchairs: Accommodated
Helpers: Admitted
Prices: Normal prices apply for the disabled and helpers
Disabled Toilets: None
Contact: (07815) 858404 Noel Walker
(Bookings are necessary)

Travelling Supporters' Information:
Routes: From Portadown Main Centre take the road signposted for Tandragee/Newry. Turn into Hanover Street near the railway bridge then right at the traffic lights. Follow this road round under a railway bridge and the ground is situated on the left after about ½ mile.

BALLINAMALLARD UNITED FC

Founded: 1975
Former Names: None
Nickname: 'Mallards'
Ground: Ferney Park, Ballinamallard   BT94 2EZ
Record Attendance: 1,020 (1994/95 season)
Pitch Size: 110 × 70 yards

Colours: Royal Blue shirts with White shorts
Telephone Nº: (028) 6638-8600
Ground Capacity: 4,000
Seating Capacity: 250
Web Site: None

GENERAL INFORMATION
Car Parking: Spaces for 50 cars available at the ground
Coach Parking: At the ground
Nearest Railway Station: None nearby
Nearest Bus Station: Ballinamallard (½ mile)
Club Shop: In the Social Club
Opening Times: Tuesday to Saturday 8.00pm to 11.30pm and Sundays 3.00pm to 11.00pm
Telephone Nº: –

ADMISSION INFO (2005/2006 PRICES)
Adult Standing: £3.00
Adult Seating: £3.00
Senior Citizen/Junior Standing: £2.00
Senior Citizen/Junior Seating: £2.00
Programme Price: £1.50

DISABLED INFORMATION
Wheelchairs: Accommodated
Helpers: Admitted
Prices: Normal prices apply for the disabled and helpers
Disabled Toilets: Available in the Clubhouse
Contact: (028) 6638-8600   (Bookings are not necessary)

Travelling Supporters' Information:
Routes: Ballinamallard is situated about 10 miles to the North of Enniskillen on the B46. The ground is ¼ mile to the south of the village.

BRANTWOOD FC

Founded: 1901
Former Names: None
Nickname: 'Brants'
Ground: Skegoneill Park, Skegoneill Avenue, Belfast, BT15 3JR
Record Attendance: Not known
Pitch Size: 108 × 72 yards

Colours: Royal Blue shirts and shorts
Telephone Nº: (028) 9077-2370
Ground Capacity: 2,000
Seating Capacity: None
Web Site: www.brantwoodfc.com

GENERAL INFORMATION

Car Parking: At the ground
Coach Parking: At the ground
Nearest Railway Station: Belfast York Road
Nearest Bus Station: Belfast Laganside
Club Shop: None
Opening Times: –
Telephone Nº: –

ADMISSION INFO (2005/2006 PRICES)

Adult Standing: £3.00
Adult Seating: £3.00
Senior Citizen/Junior Standing: £1.00
Senior Citizen/Junior Seating: £1.00
Programme Price: £1.50

DISABLED INFORMATION

Wheelchairs: Accommodated
Helpers: Admitted
Prices: Free of charge for the disabled and helpers
Disabled Toilets: Available
Contact: (028) 9077-2370   (Bookings are not necessary)

Travelling Supporters' Information:
Routes: Exit the M2 at Junction 1 and take the Shore Road southwards. Pass Crusaders FC Seaview Ground then turn right into Skegoneill Avenue and the ground is on the left at the junction with Jellicoe Avenue.

CHIMNEY CORNER FC

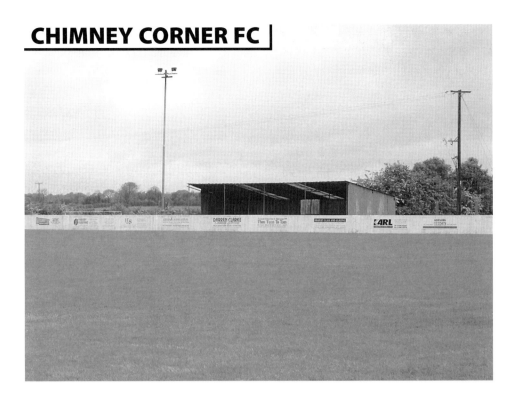

Founded: 1952
Former Names: None
Nickname: 'The Corner'
Ground: Allen Park, Randalstown Road, Antrim
Record Attendance: 900
Pitch Size: 114 × 76 yards

Colours: Red shirts with Black shorts
Telephone Nº: (028) 9446-1256
Ground Capacity: 2,000
Seating Capacity: None
Web Site: None

GENERAL INFORMATION
Car Parking: At the ground
Coach Parking: At the ground
Nearest Railway Station: Antrim
Nearest Bus Station: Antrim
Club Shop: None
Opening Times: –
Telephone Nº: –

ADMISSION INFO (2005/2006 PRICES)
Adult Standing: £4.00
Senior Citizen/Junior Standing: £2.00
Programme Price: None

DISABLED INFORMATION
Wheelchairs: Accommodated
Helpers: Admitted
Prices: £2.00 each for helpers and the disabled
Disabled Toilets: Available
Contact: (028) 9446-1256   (Bookings are necessary)

Travelling Supporters' Information:
Routes: Take the A6 to Antrim town centre. Turn right at the traffic lights by the Police Station and turn left at the roundabout into Randalstown Road. Continue for about 1 mile and the ground is situated on the right after the Rugby Ground.

DERGVIEW FC

Founded: 1980
Former Names: None
Nickname: None
Ground: Darragh Park, Castlegore Road, Castlederg
Record Attendance: Not known
Pitch Size: 105 × 65 yards

Colours: Black and White striped shirts, Black shorts
Contact Telephone Nº: (07759) 933505
Ground Capacity: 1,000
Seating Capacity: None
Web Site: None

GENERAL INFORMATION
Car Parking: At the ground
Coach Parking: At the ground
Nearest Railway Station: –
Nearest Bus Station: Strabane
Club Shop: None
Opening Times: –
Telephone Nº: –

ADMISSION INFO (2005/2006 PRICES)
Adult Standing: £3.00
Senior Citizen/Junior Standing: £1.00
Programme Price: None

DISABLED INFORMATION
Wheelchairs: Accommodated
Helpers: Admitted
Prices: Normal prices apply for the disabled and helpers
Disabled Toilets: Available
Contact: (07759) 933505 – Margaret Doherty
(Bookings are not necessary)

Travelling Supporters' Information:
Routes: Take the A5 from Strabane towards Omagh and then the B72 just before Victoria Bridge towards Castlederg. Pass through Castlederg over the bridge and the ground is down a track on the right opposite Castlederg High School.

LURGAN CELTIC FC

Founded: 1903
Former Names: None
Nickname: 'Hoops'
Ground: Knockramer Park, Silverwood Road, Lurgan
Record Attendance: Not known
Pitch Size: 110 × 71 yards

Colours: Green & White hooped shirts, White shorts
Telephone Nº: (07840) 284383
Ground Capacity: 1,000
Seating Capacity: None (100 planned)
Web Site: www.lurgancelticfc.com

GENERAL INFORMATION

Car Parking: Street parking only
Coach Parking: Street parking only
Nearest Railway Station: Lurgan (1½ miles)
Nearest Bus Station: Craigavon (3 miles)
Club Shop: None
Opening Times: –
Telephone Nº: –

ADMISSION INFO (2005/2006 PRICES)

Adult Standing: £3.00
Senior Citizen/Junior Standing: £1.00
Programme Price: None

DISABLED INFORMATION

Wheelchairs: Accommodated
Helpers: Admitted
Prices: Normal prices apply for the disabled and helpers
Disabled Toilets: Available
Contact: (07840) 284383 (Bookings are necessary)

Travelling Supporters' Information:
Routes: Take the Lurgan turn-off from the M1 (Junction 10) and travel along the A26. Turn right at the first set of traffic lights and continue to the T-junction. Turn right and the ground is on the right after ¼ mile.

OXFORD UNITED STARS FC

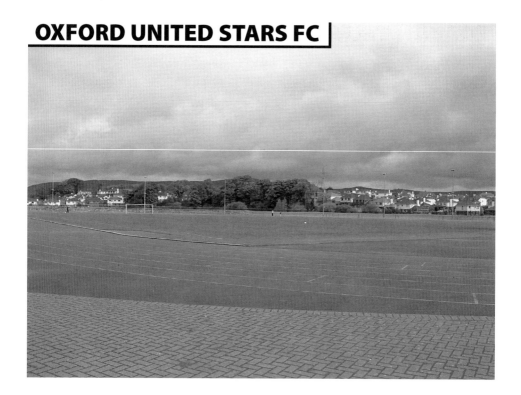

Founded: Not known
Former Names: None
Nickname: 'Stars'
Ground: Templemore Sports Complex, Buncrana Road, Londonderry   BT48 7QL
Record Attendance: Not known
Pitch Size: 110 × 71 yards

Colours: Blue and White striped shirts, Black shorts
Telephone Nº: (028) 7126-8637 – Mr. Crampsie
Contact Address: Jim Gallagher, 22 Little Diamond, Londonderry   BT48 9ED
Telephone Nº: (028) 7136-4128
Ground Capacity: 1,500
Seating Capacity: None

GENERAL INFORMATION
Car Parking: At the ground
Coach Parking: At the ground
Nearest Railway Station: Waterside (3 miles)
Nearest Bus Station: Londonderry City Centre (2 miles)
Club Shop: None
Opening Times: –
Telephone Nº: –

ADMISSION INFO (2005/2006 PRICES)
Adult Standing: £2.00
Senior Citizen/Junior Standing: £2.00
Programme Price: None

DISABLED INFORMATION
Wheelchairs: Accommodated
Helpers: Admitted
Prices: Normal prices apply
Disabled Toilets: Available
Contact: – (Bookings are not necessary)

Travelling Supporters' Information:
Routes: Templemore Sports Complex is situated on the western outskirts of Londonderry on the A2. Come along the Buncrana Road and it is clearly marked on the right.

PORTSTEWART FC

Founded: 1968
Former Names: None
Nickname: 'Seahawks'
Ground: Seahaven, St. John's Close, Portstewart
Record Attendance: Not known
Pitch Size: 105 × 65 yards

Colours: Sky Blue shirts with Navy Blue shorts
Telephone N°: (028) 7083-5111
Ground Capacity: 1,000
Seating Capacity: None
Web Site: None

GENERAL INFORMATION
Car Parking: At the ground
Coach Parking: At the ground
Nearest Railway Station: Portstewart (½ mile)
Nearest Bus Station: Coleraine (3 miles)
Club Shop: None
Opening Times: –
Telephone N°: –

ADMISSION INFO (2005/2006 PRICES)
Adult Standing: £3.00
Senior Citizen Standing: £1.50
Junior Standing: Free of charge
Programme Price: None

DISABLED INFORMATION
Wheelchairs: Accommodated
Helpers: Admitted
Prices: Normal prices apply for the disabled and helpers
Disabled Toilets: Available
Contact: – (Bookings are not necessary)

Travelling Supporters' Information:
Routes: Head for Coleraine and follow the Portrush signs around the ring road to the roundabout at the end and take the 1st exit to Portstewart (B185). Pass through Portstewart along the main street by the harbour and head back towards Coleraine on the A2. After the mini-roundabout take the 1st exit on the left into St. John's Close and the ground is along on the right.

PSNI FC

> No Ground Photograph was available
> at the time of going to press

Founded: 1956
Former Names: Royal Ulster Constabulary FC
Nickname: 'Police'
Ground: 18B Newforge Lane, Belfast   BT9 5NW
Record Attendance: Not known
Pitch Size: 110 × 70 yards

Colours: Green, Red and Black shirts with Black shorts
Telephone Nº: –
Ground Capacity: 1,500
Seating Capacity: None
Web Site: None

GENERAL INFORMATION
Car Parking: At the ground
Coach Parking: At the ground
Nearest Railway Station: Belfast Central
Nearest Bus Station: Victoria Street, Belfast
Club Shop: None
Opening Times: –

ADMISSION INFO (2005/2006 PRICES)
Adult Standing: £3.00
Senior Citizen/Junior Standing: £2.00
Programme Price: None

DISABLED INFORMATION
Wheelchairs: Accommodated
Helpers: Admitted
Prices: Normal prices apply for the disabled and helpers
Disabled Toilets: Available

Travelling Supporters' Information:
Routes: From the City Centre: Take University Road into Malone Road and turn left into Newforge Lane. The ground is on the left, almost at the end of Newforge Lane and is signposted for Newforge Country Club.

QUEENS UNIVERSITY FC

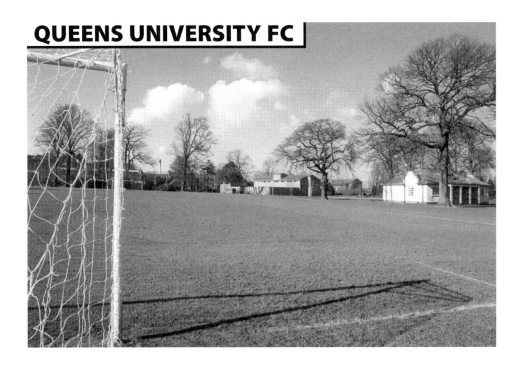

Founded: 1900
Former Names: None
Nickname: 'Queens'
Ground: Newforge Lane, Belfast
Record Attendance: Not known
Pitch Size: 110 × 71 yards

Colours: White shirts with Black shorts
Telephone Nº: (028) 9068-1027
Ground Capacity: 1,000
Seating Capacity: None
Web Site: None

GENERAL INFORMATION
Car Parking: At the ground
Coach Parking: At the ground
Nearest Railway Station: Belfast Central
Nearest Bus Station: Victoria Street, Belfast
Club Shop: None
Opening Times: –
Telephone Nº: –

ADMISSION INFO (2005/2006 PRICES)
Adult Standing: £2.00
Senior Citizen/Junior Standing: £1.00
Programme Price: None

DISABLED INFORMATION
Wheelchairs: Accommodated
Helpers: Admitted
Prices: Normal prices apply for the disabled and helpers
Disabled Toilets: Available nearby
Contact: (028) 9068-1027   (Bookings are necessary)

Travelling Supporters' Information:
Routes: From the City Centre: Take University Road into Malone Road and turn left into Newforge Lane.

WAKEHURST FC

Founded: 1969
Former Names: None
Nickname: None
Ground: The Showgrounds, Pitch Two, Warden Street, Ballymena   BT43 7DR
Record Attendance: 150
Pitch Size: 105 × 70 yards

Colours: Black and White striped shirts, Black shorts
Telephone Nº: (028) 2563-8510
Ground Capacity: 300
Seating Capacity: None
Web Site: www.get.to/wakehurstfc

GENERAL INFORMATION
Car Parking: At the ground
Coach Parking: At the ground
Nearest Railway Station: Ballymena (1 mile)
Nearest Bus Station: Ballymena (1 mile)
Club Shop: None
Opening Times: –
Telephone Nº: –

ADMISSION INFO (2005/2006 PRICES)
Adult Standing: £3.00
Senior Citizen/Junior Standing: £2.00
Programme Price: None

DISABLED INFORMATION
Wheelchairs: Accommodated
Helpers: Admitted
Prices: Normal prices apply for the disabled and helpers
Disabled Toilets: None
Contact: –   (Bookings are not necessary)

Travelling Supporters' Information:
Routes: Take the A26 into Ballymena. In the Town Centre, at the junction of the A42 and A43, turn off at the roundabout into Warden Street. The ground is situated at the end of the road after about ¼ mile.

Irish Premier League 2004/2005 Season	Ards	Ballymena United	Cliftonville	Coleraine	Crusaders	Dungannon Swifts	Glentoran	Institute	Larne	Limavady United	Linfield	Lisburn Distillery	Loughgall	Newry City	Omagh Town	Portadown
Ards	■	1-1	1-3	1-2	2-2	1-3	0-3	1-2	0-3	0-1	2-2	0-1	0-0	5-1	2-0	0-1
Ballymena United	2-2	■	1-1	2-2	1-1	1-2	0-3	1-1	0-0	2-1	3-4	2-1	2-1	2-1	1-1	2-0
Cliftonville	0-3	0-0	■	1-4	1-0	1-1	0-1	1-0	2-0	0-2	0-0	1-0	1-3	0-1	2-1	0-2
Coleraine	3-0	0-2	3-1	■	1-1	4-2	0-1	2-4	3-0	1-2	0-4	1-3	2-0	6-1	3-4	2-2
Crusaders	0-2	2-3	0-2	1-1	■	0-3	0-2	1-0	1-1	1-0	1-2	0-0	3-2	0-1	3-1	0-1
Dungannon Swifts	7-0	1-2	3-1	0-1	0-0	■	2-0	3-0	3-1	1-1	1-1	1-1	1-0	1-0	2-1	1-3
Glentoran	2-0	4-2	4-0	1-0	4-1	5-0	■	2-0	3-0	2-0	3-2	1-0	2-0	3-1	3-0	1-2
Institute	1-1	1-1	1-2	3-1	2-0	3-2	0-1	■	3-0	0-3	0-1	1-3	3-0	2-1	0-1	2-1
Larne	2-2	0-0	0-0	1-5	5-2	3-2	0-5	2-0	■	0-4	0-2	0-0	2-3	0-1	2-0	2-3
Limavady United	0-1	2-1	0-0	0-3	1-1	3-2	2-2	5-1	6-0	■	0-1	2-2	1-1	3-2	2-0	0-2
Linfield	3-0	0-1	3-1	4-1	2-1	2-1	1-1	3-1	1-1	4-1	■	5-2	3-0	2-0	6-1	0-0
Lisburn Distillery	1-1	0-2	3-1	2-2	3-2	2-0	2-1	3-2	2-1	1-1	0-4	■	3-1	1-3	6-1	2-0
Loughgall	3-1	1-0	0-0	1-5	2-0	1-2	1-3	0-1	0-2	1-1	0-4	2-1	■	1-1	1-3	0-2
Newry City	1-0	1-1	4-2	0-1	2-0	0-4	0-4	4-1	1-3	2-2	0-3	0-0	2-5	■	2-1	0-6
Omagh Town	2-1	0-2	0-5	1-3	1-3	1-4	2-3	0-1	3-0	2-5	1-8	2-3	0-2	2-2	■	1-2
Portadown	2-3	3-0	3-0	2-0	0-0	1-2	4-3	4-0	3-0	0-1	0-1	2-1	2-2	2-3	9-0	■

Irish Premier League

Season 2004/2005

Glentoran	30	24	2	4	73	22	74
Linfield	30	22	6	2	78	23	72
Portadown	30	18	4	8	64	29	58
Dungannon Swifts	30	15	5	10	57	40	50
Limavady United	30	13	9	8	52	36	48
Coleraine	30	14	5	11	62	47	47
Lisburn Distillery	30	13	8	9	49	42	47
Ballymena United	30	11	12	7	40	37	45
Institute	30	11	3	16	36	50	36
Newry City	30	10	5	15	38	63	35
Cliftonville	30	9	7	14	29	44	34
Loughgall	30	8	6	16	34	53	30
Larne	30	7	7	16	31	60	28
Ards	30	6	8	16	33	54	26
Crusaders	30	5	9	16	27	48	24
Omagh Town	30	5	2	23	33	88	17

Promotion/Relegation Play-off

Glenavon	1	Crusaders	1
Crusaders	1	Glenavon	2

Glenavon won 3-2 on aggregate and won promotion as a result

Champions: Glentoran
Relegated: Crusaders and Omagh Town

Irish Football League First Division 2004/2005 Season	Armagh City	Ballinamallard United	Ballyclare Comrades	Ballymoney United	Bangor	Carrick Rangers	Coagh United	Donegal Celtic	Dundela	Glenavon	Harland & Wolff Welders	Moyola Park
Armagh City		3-0	1-0	1-0	3-2	3-0	1-1	2-1	1-1	3-1	1-0	2-0
Ballinamallard United	1-2		2-0	4-3	1-2	2-0	2-5	0-0	0-3	1-3	0-1	0-0
Ballyclare Comrades	1-1	1-0		1-1	0-0	0-0	2-1	0-3	1-1	0-1	2-4	2-0
Ballymoney United	0-1	1-0	0-4		0-2	4-3	4-3	2-1	3-1	0-1	0-1	0-1
Bangor	1-1	2-0	0-0	4-0		0-2	3-2	0-2	0-1	1-1	1-3	1-0
Carrick Rangers	0-0	2-0	1-2	3-1	2-0		0-2	1-2	2-3	4-2	1-1	0-1
Coagh United	1-2	3-0	1-1	0-3	1-1	2-0		1-1	1-1	0-3	2-4	2-0
Donegal Celtic	0-0	0-0	1-0	3-1	3-0	5-0	1-3		1-2	0-2	3-0	0-0
Dundela	1-3	2-0	1-2	3-2	1-4	0-1	2-2	1-2		0-3	1-1	0-0
Glenavon	0-2	4-0	1-0	5-1	1-2	3-0	6-1	1-1	2-0		1-0	3-0
Harland & Wolff Welders	1-1	3-2	3-1	3-3	3-3	1-1	2-3	1-0	1-0	0-1		1-0
Moyola Park	0-1	2-0	1-2	1-0	2-2	3-2	1-2	2-4	1-3	1-1	2-1	

Irish Football League – First Division

Season 2004/2005

Armagh City	22	15	7	0	35	11	52
Glenavon	22	14	4	4	43	17	46
Donegal Celtic	22	10	6	6	34	19	36
Harland & Wolff Welders	22	10	6	6	35	29	36
Bangor	22	9	6	7	33	29	33
Coagh United	22	8	5	9	39	42	29
Ballyclare Comrades	22	7	7	8	22	24	28
Dundela	22	7	6	9	28	33	27
Moyola Park	22	6	5	11	18	29	23
Carrick Rangers	22	6	4	12	25	37	22
Ballymoney United	22	6	2	14	29	45	20
Ballinamallard United	22	3	4	15	14	40	13

Promoted: Armagh City & Glenavon
Relegated: Ballinamallard United

Irish Football League Second Division 2004/2005 Season	Annagh United	Banbridge Town	Brantwood	Chimney Corner	Dergview	Lurgan Celtic	Oxford United Stars	PSNI	Portstewart	Queens University	Tobermore United	Wakehurst
Annagh United		0-5	1-1	3-3	1-3	1-1	1-1	1-2	2-1	3-1	1-0	1-0
Banbridge Town	0-2		2-1	5-1	5-2	3-0	4-1	1-1	2-1	4-0	2-1	1-1
Brantwood	4-3	2-0		1-2	2-2	0-4	2-2	2-1	1-1	2-2	1-3	0-3
Chimney Corner	1-1	0-0	2-2		2-3	4-4	2-0	0-1	0-2	4-3	1-2	0-0
Dergview	0-2	1-3	2-1	1-3		0-2	1-1	2-0	2-3	6-6	2-1	1-2
Lurgan Celtic	1-3	2-1	4-0	3-0	3-1		2-1	0-1	0-0	1-1	2-3	3-2
Oxford United Stars	1-1	0-3	2-1	0-2	2-1	1-3		3-0	0-2	1-1	2-1	1-1
PSNI	4-0	2-2	3-2	0-2	1-1	2-2	1-0		4-2	1-1	0-3	1-1
Portstewart	0-3	0-1	1-1	0-0	0-2	1-1	2-0	1-0		2-0	3-2	0-1
Queens University	1-0	0-1	3-3	0-0	0-3	3-3	1-4	0-1	0-3		0-3	2-2
Tobermore United	1-0	2-1	2-1	4-0	4-2	3-2	3-0	2-1	2-0	3-1		1-3
Wakehurst	1-2	2-2	3-0	1-2	1-1	3-2	1-2	1-0	1-1	2-1	1-1	

Irish Football League – Second Division

Season 2004/2005

Tobermore United	22	15	1	6	47	26	46
Banbridge Town	22	13	5	4	48	22	44
Lurgan Celtic	22	9	7	6	45	34	34
Wakehurst	22	8	9	5	34	26	33
Annagh United	22	9	6	7	32	32	33
Porstewart	22	8	6	8	26	25	30
PSNI	22	8	6	8	27	29	30
Chimney Corner	22	7	8	7	31	36	29
Dergview	22	7	5	10	39	45	26
Oxford United Stars	22	6	6	10	25	36	24
Brantwood	22	4	7	11	30	46	19
Queens University	22	1	8	13	25	52	11

Promoted: Tobermore United & Banbridge Town

49

Ards FC
2004-2005 Season Statistics

1	Sep	25	A	Institute	D	1-1	Fitzgerald 34'
2	Oct	2	A	Cliftonville	W	3-0	Kennedy 27' 76' 83'
3		9	A	Coleraine	L	0-3	
4		16	H	Glentoran	L	0-3	
5		23	A	Crusaders	W	2-0	Reddish 8', Delany 57'
6		30	H	Linfield	D	2-2	Kennedy 8' (pen), Fitzgerald 53'
7	Nov	6	A	Limavady United	W	1-0	Kennedy 29'
8		13	A	Ballymena United	D	2-2	Kennedy 58' (pen), Cleary 83'
9		20	H	Omagh Town	W	2-0	Fitzgerald 23', Kennedy 87'
10		27	H	Portadown	L	0-1	
11	Dec	4	A	Lisburn Distillery	D	1-1	Kennedy 82'
12		14	H	Loughgall	D	0-0	
13		17	A	Newry City	L	0-1	
14		27	H	Larne	L	0-3	
15	Jan	1	A	Dungannon Swifts	L	0-7	
16		8	H	Cliftonville	L	1-3	Kennedy 75'
17		22	H	Coleraine	L	1-2	Fairclough 69'
18		29	A	Glentoran	L	0-2	
19	Feb	1	H	Institute	L	1-2	Ward 73'
20		5	H	Crusaders	D	2-2	Campbell 14' (pen), Bailie 47'
21		19	A	Linfield	L	0-3	
22		26	H	Limavady United	L	0-1	
23	Mar	12	H	Ballymena United	D	1-1	Rainey 13'
24		19	A	Omagh Town	L	1-2	Kennedy 11'
25		24	A	Portadown	W	3-2	Kennedy 56', Rainey 80', Waterworth 90'
26		29	H	Lisburn Distillery	L	0-1	
27	Apr	9	A	Loughgall	L	1-3	Fairclough 4'
28		16	H	Dungannon Swifts	L	1-3	Watson 71'
29		23	A	Larne	D	2-2	Kennedy 9', Waterworth 81'
30		30	H	Newry City	W	5-1	Rainey 14' 36' 38', Kennedy 54' 90'

Final League Position: 14th in the Irish Premier League

Appearances

Sub. Appearances

Goals

S. Robertson	J. Bailie	K. Pike	A. Watson	P. Gollogley	M. Hunter	S. Cleary	D. Delany	G. Kennedy	D. Fitzgerald	D. Rainey	D. Murphy	S. Reddish	M. Lawless	A. Fox	S. McCrory	R. Campbell	K. Dougherty	A. Rees	T. McVea	R. Scannell	S. O'Shaughnessy	I. Forsythe	A. Murray	I. McDonagh	D. Ward	D. Fairclough	R. Cathcart	D. Wilton	A. Waterworth	R. Knox	C. McCreery	
1	2	3	4°	5	6†	7	8	9	10	11	12*	14†	15°																			1
	2	3	7	5	10		11	9			4			1	6	8																2
	2	3	10	5	9*	7	11†				4	12*		1	6	8	14†															3
	2	3	5	10		7	12*	9*		11	4			1	6	8	14†															4
	2	3	8	5	4	7	11	10						6	1			9														5
	3	2	5	4	7	11*	9	10				12*			1	8		6														6
1	3	2*		4			11	9		10	7	12*			6	8			5													7
1	3			5	7		11	9		10	2				6*	8†	14†		4	12*												8
1	12*	3		5	7†		11	9		10	2*					8	14†		4	6												9
1	14†	3	4	5	2†		11	9		10	12*					8				6*												10
1	2	3	8	5	7*	12*	11†	9		10							14†		4	6												11
	2	3		5	4	7	11†	9	12*			8			1		14†	10*		6												12
	2*	3		5		7	11	9		10†					1	8	12*		4	6		14†										13
	2*	3					11			10†		14†			1	5	8	7		4	6	9	12*									14
		3					11†	9		10		7			1	5°	8	2		4	6	12*	15°	14†								15
1		3				7		9		10						8*	11	2		4	6		12*	5								16
1		3	5	7				10		4						8		2		6					9	11						17
1	2	3	7	5	8			12*		9*								6†						4	10	11						18
	2	3		5	7*	12*		9°		11†						8	14†			6				4	10		15°	1				19
	2*	3	11	5	4	7										8				6				9	12*			1	10			20
1	2	3	4	5	11†	*		10°		15°						8				6				9	12*				14†			21
	2	3		14†	10	7									1	8				6					11†	5	4		9*	12*		22
	2		5		11			9		10					1	8				6			3				4		7			23
	2	14†	3		4			9		10					1	8*				6				5†	12*	11			7			24
	2	3	7		6			9		11					1	8									12*	5	4		10	14†		25
	2	3	7		6			9		11†					1	8*	14†			6					12*	4	5		10			26
	2	3†	8*	11				9		14†					1	12*				6				7		4	5		10			27
1	2	3°	11	5		7		12*		9						8*				6						4	15°		14†	10†		28
1	2	3	7	5	11			9		10						8				6						4*			12*			29
1	2	3	7	5*	11	12*		9		10°						8†				6						4			14†		15°	30
13	22	28	20	17	25	13	14	25	8	20	3	2	0	15	7	23	4	6	7	20	1			5	7	11	4	2	7	1		Apps
	2	1			1	3	1	2	1	6	2	1	2			1	5	2		2	2	2	2		3	2	3		4	2	1	Subs
		1		1		1	1	14	3	5		1				1									1	2			2			Goals

51

Ballymena United FC
2004-2005 Season Statistics

1	Sep	25	A	Loughgall	L	0-1	
2	Oct	2	H	Newry City	W	2-1	McLaughlin 37' (og), Simms 90'
3		9	A	Dungannon Swifts	W	2-1	Hill 31', Simms 90'
4		16	H	Institute	D	1-1	Hill 61'
5		23	A	Linfield	W	1-0	Melly 27'
6		30	H	Crusaders	D	1-1	McCann 90'
7	Nov	6	A	Portadown	L	0-3	
8		13	H	Ards	D	2-2	Simms 17', Smyth 87'
9		20	A	Limavady United	L	1-2	McBride 71'
10		27	A	Lisburn Distillery	W	2-0	Melly 5', Scates 71'
11	Dec	4	H	Omagh Town	D	1-1	McBride 80'
12		11	H	Cliftonville	D	1-1	Adams 4' (og)
13		18	A	Larne	D	0-0	
14		27	H	Coleraine	D	2-2	Hill 34', McBride 57'
15	Jan	3	H	Loughgall	W	2-1	Smyth 65', Kearney 75'
16		18	A	Glentoran	L	2-4	Boyd 11', Fitzgerald 64'
17		22	H	Dungannon Swifts	L	1-2	Hamill 11'
18		29	A	Institute	D	1-1	Hill 78'
19	Feb	5	H	Linfield	L	3-4	Mullan 28', Smyth 74', Watson 90'
20		19	A	Crusaders	W	3-2	Nolan 30' 46', Kearney 34'
21		26	H	Portadown	W	2-0	Smyth 58', Fitzgerald 73'
22	Mar	1	A	Newry City	D	1-1	Nolan 90'
23		12	A	Ards	D	1-1	Fitzgerald 8'
24		19	H	Limavady United	W	2-1	Mullan 1', Watson 75'
25		24	H	Lisburn Distillery	W	2-1	Kearney 39', Mullan 50'
26		29	A	Omagh Town	W	2-0	Hamill 30', Kearney 55'
27	Apr	9	A	Cliftonville	D	0-0	
28		16	H	Glentoran	L	0-3	
29		23	A	Coleraine	W	2-0	Watson 36', Mullan 57'
30		30	H	Larne	D	0-0	

Final League Position: 8th in the Irish Premier League

Appearances
Sub. Appearances
Goals

R. Robinson	G. Simms	C. Donaghy	A. Watson	J. Marks	G. Smyth	T. McCann	O. Kearney	S. Campbell	R. Hamill	J. McBride	J. Gray	M. Hughes	G. Scates	E. Hill	D. Melly	N. Boyd	W. McFrederick	A. Rosbotham	G. McCabe	D. Fitzgerald	G. Mullan	D. Youle	M. Nolan	R. Reid	
1	2†	3	4	5	6	7	8	9	10	11*	12*	14†													1
1	5	3	4		6		8°	12*	10†		9	11*	2	7	14†	15°									2
	4	2*	5	10		12*			6				8	9	7	3	1	11							3
	4*	3	5	2	12*			15°	6		7°		8	9†	10	11	1	14†							4
		2	5	10	6	7*		12*			4		8	9†	11	3	1	14†							5
	14†	2	5	10	6	12*	11		8		4*			9†	7	3°	1	15°							6
	12*	3	5	10°	6	7	4*		8		2		15°	8	14†		1	11†							7
	9	3	5		6	7	8			10*	4		2	11	12*		1								8
	9	3	5		6	7	8†		12*		10	4*	2	11°	14†	15°	1								9
1		2	5		6	7			9		10		4	11	3										10
1		2	5		6	7*	14†		9		10		4	8	11	3				12†					11
1	6	3	5				8		7		10		4	2	9*	11				12*					12
1	6	2	5	10	12*		8						4	9	7	11			3*						13
1	6	3	5†	10	14†		8		4	9			2		7*	11		12*							14
1	5	3		10	6		8		4†	14†			2	7†	12*	11						9			15
	5	3*		10	6		8		7	14†	2		4		12*	11	1	9†							16
1	14†	3	5	10	6*		8		7	9†	2		4	12*		11									17
1	2	3	5	10	6		8						4	12*	7†			14†	9	11*					18
1		3	5		6		8		14†		7		4	12°*	15°					10†	11*	2	9		19
1	6	3	5				8						4		7					10	11	2	9		20
1	5	3	2		6		8						4		7					10	11		9		21
1	5	3	2		6*		8		12*	10			4		7						11		9		22
1	6	3	5				8		7		4		2			11				10*	12*		9		23
1	5	3	2		6		8		14†	12*	4*				7	11†					10		9		24
1	5	3	2		6		8		14†		4			12*	7	11					10†		9*		25
1	5	3	2	15°			8		6		4		14†	9	7°	11*		12*			10†				26
1	5	3	2†	12*	6		8		9		7		4	14†		11*					10				27
1	5	3	2*	12*	6		8		10		7†		4	14†	15°	11					9				28
1	15°	3	5	2	6		8		12*				4†	14†	7	11°					10		9*		29
1		3	5	2	6		8		10					12*	7						11*	4	9†	14†	30
22	21	30	28	14	22	7	25	1	17	9	19	2	22	13	18	18	8	2	1	7	12	3	9	0	Apps
	4		3	3	1	2	2		6	13	2	1	2	8	8	2		7	1		1			1	Subs
	3		3		4	1	4		2	3			1	4	2	1					3	4	3		Goals

Cliftonville FC
2004-2005 Season Statistics

#	Month	Date	H/A	Opponent	Result	Score	Scorers
1	Sep	25	H	Lisburn Distillery	W	1-0	Scannell 52'
2	Oct	2	H	Ards	L	0-3	
3		9	H	Omagh Town	W	2-1	Scannell 6', Friars 35'
4		16	A	Portadown	L	0-3	
5		23	H	Glentoran	L	0-1	
6		29	A	Newry City	L	2-4	O'Loughlin 42', Scannell 58'
7	Nov	6	H	Coleraine	L	1-4	O'Loughlin 24'
8		13	A	Dungannon Swifts	L	1-3	C. McMullan 90'
9		20	A	Loughgall	D	0-0	
10		26	H	Institute	W	1-0	Friars 64'
11	Dec	4	H	Larne	W	2-0	Fleming 68', Friars 81' (pen)
12		11	A	Ballymena United	D	1-1	C. McMullan 45'
13		18	H	Linfield	D	0-0	
14		27	A	Crusaders	W	2-0	Mulvenna 6', Crawford 79'
15	Jan	3	A	Lisburn Distillery	L	1-3	Cunning 19'
16		8	A	Ards	W	3-1	McConnell 64' 85', Mulvenna 70'
17		22	A	Omagh Town	W	5-0	McConnell 9', Crawford 37' 70', Hennigan 59', O'Loughlin 62'
18		29	H	Portadown	L	0-2	
19	Feb	5	A	Glentoran	L	0-4	
20		19	H	Newry City	L	0-1	
21		26	A	Coleraine	L	1-3	Friars 63' (pen)
22	Mar	2	H	Limavady United	L	0-2	
23		12	H	Dungannon Swifts	D	1-1	Friars 54'
24		19	H	Loughgall	L	1-3	Friars 11'
25		24	A	Institute	W	2-1	C. McLaughlin 30' (og), Downey 51'
26		28	A	Larne	D	0-0	
27	Apr	9	H	Ballymena United	D	0-0	
28		16	A	Limavady United	D	0-0	
29		23	H	Crusaders	W	1-0	Telford 37'
30		30	A	Linfield	L	1-3	McElroy 28'

Final League Position: 11th in the Irish Premier League

Appearances

Sub. Appearances

Goals

P. Straney	L. Fleming	G. McMullan	K. Mulvenna	S. Adams	J. O'Loughlin	N. McConnell	C. McMullan	C. Scannell	C. Downey	S. Friars	S. Hennigan	C. Brannigan	P. Bradley	E. Mapp	W. Beckett	A. Crawford	D. O'Hara	M. Farrell	A. Young	C. Toye	G. Campbell	P. McKane	B. Cunning	G. Treanor	W. Loughran	J. McElroy	J. Connolly	P. Telford	R. Kerr	
1	2	3	4	5	6†	7°	8	9	10*	11	12*	14†	15°																	1
1	2	3	4	5	6*	7	8°	9	10	11†	12*	14†	5°																	2
	2	8*	4	5	6	7°		9	10	11	12*	3†		1	14†	15°														3
	2	6	4	5		7		9		11*	8†	3		1	12*	10°	14†	15°												4
	2		4	5	6*	7°	8	9	10	11†	12*	3			14†				1	15°										5
	2	7	4	5	6	12*	8*	9	10	11†		3		1		14†														6
	2	9	4	15°	6°	7	8			11	10†	3*			14†		5		1		12*									7
	2	9	4	12*	6*	7	8			10†	11°				14†	15°	5		1		3									8
1	2	8	4	5	6	7			12*	10	11					9*					3									9
1	2	9	4	5	6†	7	8*		10	11					14†	12*					3									10
1	2	9	4		6	7	8		10*	11	12*						5				3									11
1	2	9	4	5	6	7	8		10†	11*					14†	12*					3									12
1	2	9	4	12*	6	7	8†		10	11*					14†		5				3									13
	2	8	4		6	7			10		11				12*	9*	5				3	1								14
1	2	8	4	14†	6	7°			10							9	5				3†		11*	12*	15°					15
1	2		4		6	7			10†	11					14†	9	5				3		8*	12*						16
1	2		4		6	7			10†	11	12*				14†	9	5°				3		8*		15°					17
	2		4		6	7	8*		10†	11					14†	9	5				3						1	12*		18
1	2	9	4		6	7	8°		10	11†					14†		5				3*				15°			12*		19
1	2	8	4		6†	7			10	11					14†	9	5				3*							12*		20
1		8	4		6°	7			10	11	12*				14†	9†	5				3*		15°		2					21
1	2	8	4	15°	6†	7			10	11*	12*					9	5				3°				14†					22
1	2	8	4	5	6	7*		9	10	11											3							12*		23
1	2	8	4	5	6	7			10	11						9†	5				3*				14†			12*		24
1		8		12*	6	7°			10	11					14†		5				3				2	4		9*		25
1	2	8			6	7			10	11							5				3		12*			4		9*		26
1	2	8			6	7			10	11							5				3			12*		4*		9†	14†	27
1	2	8			6	7			10	11							5				3					4		9*	12*	28
1	2	7			6		8			11							5				3		12*		14†	4		9*	10†	29
1	2	7			6		8*		10	11							5				3		12*			4		9†	14†	30
22	27	27	27	12	28	24	11	6	26	29	11	5		3	1	8	17		3		19	1	4	0	3	8	1	3	1	Apps
				6	1	1	3				11	2	2		10	4	3	2		3	2			2	3	3			5	Subs
		1			3	3	2	3	1	6	1					3							1			1		1		Goals

Coleraine FC
2004-2005 Season Statistics

1	Sep	25	H	Crusaders	D	1-1	Moon 64'
2	Oct	2	A	Lisburn Distillery	D	2-2	Fulton 59', Johnston 75'
3		9	H	Ards	W	3-0	Carson 34', Moon 44', Armstrong 74'
4		16	A	Linfield	L	1-4	Curran 82'
5		23	H	Dungannon Swifts	W	4-2	Tolan 83', Carson 51', Armstrong 80' 88'
6		30	A	Glentoran	L	0-1	
7	Nov	6	A	Cliftonville	W	4-1	Flynn 3', Moon 9', Tolan 17', Armstrong 54'
8		12	H	Larne	W	3-0	Tolan 31', Armstrong 51', McAllister 71'
9		20	A	Institute	L	1-3	Tolan 87'
10		27	H	Loughgall	W	2-0	Armstrong 61', Tolan 65'
11	Dec	4	A	Newry City	W	1-0	Tolan 12'
12		11	A	Portadown	L	0-2	
13		17	H	Limavady United	L	1-2	Tolan 29'
14		27	A	Ballymena United	D	2-2	Tolan 58', McAllister 77'
15	Jan	1	H	Omagh Town	L	3-4	Carson 11', Curran 73', Haveron 88' (pen)
16		3	A	Crusaders	D	1-1	Curran 20'
17		18	H	Lisburn Distillery	L	1-3	Curran 73'
18		22	A	Ards	W	2-1	Tolan 7', Curran 83'
19		29	H	Linfield	L	0-4	
20	Feb	5	A	Dungannon Swifts	W	1-0	Fulton 86'
21		19	H	Glentoran	L	0-1	
22		26	H	Cliftonville	W	3-1	Armstrong 54', Tolan 56', Carson 64'
23	Mar	11	A	Larne	W	5-1	Gaston 7' 74', Tolan 84', Fulton 89', Carson 90'
24		19	H	Institute	L	2-4	Curran 37', Beatty 66'
25		24	A	Loughgall	W	5-1	Curran 20', Johnston 44', Tolan 57' 75' 77'
26		29	H	Newry City	W	6-1	Curran 14', Tolan 28' (pen) 45', Armstrong 42' 56' 72'
27	Apr	8	H	Portadown	D	2-2	Armstrong 76' (pen), Ferry 84'
28		16	A	Omagh Town	W	3-1	Ferry 18' 64', Armstrong 52'
39		23	H	Ballymena United	L	0-2	
30		30	A	Limavady United	W	3-0	Carson 3' 77', Ferry 85'

Final League Position: 6th in the Irish Premier League

Appearances

Sub. Appearances

Goals

D. O'Hare	B. Johnston	J. Black	P. Gaston	K. McVey	S. Armstrong	B. Moon	K. O'Connor	J. Tolan	G. Haveron	S. Carson	B. Curran	B. Fulton	S. Clanachan	G. Flynn	P. McAllister	S. Beatty	J. Devine	D. Nelson	P. Spratt	D. McKee	C. Ferry	D. Boyce	
1	2	3	4°	5	6	7	8†	9	10*	11	12*	14†	15°										1
1	2			5	6		12*	14†	8	11	7†	9		4	3*	10							2
1	2			5	6	7	12*	9*	8	11				4	3	10							3
1	2			5	6	7	15°	9*	8	11	12*			4	3°	10†	14†						4
1	2°		15°	5	6	7*		9	8†	11	12*			4	3	10	14†						5
1			4	5	6	14†		9	8*	11†	7			2	3	10	12*						6
1	11		4	5†	8	7*	15°	9	14†		12*			2	3	10°	6						7
1	6		4†		8	7	14†	9*	5	11	12*			2		10	3						8
1	6†		4		8	12*	14†	9	5	11	7*			2		10	3						9
1	2†		4	5	8	7	12*	9	3*	11	14†					10	6						10
1	14†		4	5	8*	7†	6	9	12*	11	2					10	3						11
1	15°		4		8*	12*	6	9	14†	11†	7			2		10	3	5°					12
1	15°		4*	5	8	12*	14†	9	6	11	7†			2°		10	3						13
1	5		4		8	12*		9	6	11	7*			2		10	3						14
1	12*		4*	5	8†	7		9	6	11	14†			2		10	3						15
				5	12*	7	4		14†	11	8†	9*		2		10°	6		1	3	15°		16
1	12*		4	5*	9	7†	15°	14†	6	11	8°			2		10	3						17
1			4		7*	12*	6	9	5	11	8			2		10	3						18
1	6		4*		9†	14†	7		5	11	8			2		10	3			12*			19
1	12*		4		6*	7			5	11	8	9		2	3	10							20
1			4	5	8†	7		9	6	11*	12*	14†		2		10	3						21
1	6		4	5	8	7		9		11				2		10	3						22
1	8		4*	5		14†		9	10	11	7†	12*		2	3		6						23
1	6°		4*	5	12*	14†		9	10	11	7	15°		2	3†		8						24
1	6		4°	5	11	14†		9	10	12*	7†	15°		2	3*		8						25
1	6			5*	11°	14†		9	4	12*	7†	15°		2	3	10	8						26
	6		4°	2	9	15°			5*	12*	7	11†		3	10	8		1			14†		27
1	6		4	5	9°	14†			12†	11	7	15°		2	3		8*				10		28
1	6		4	5		12*				11	7	9†		2	3					8*	10	14†	29
1	6		4°	5		14†			10	11	7†	12*		2	3		8*			15°	9		30
28	20	1	24	23	25	14	6	21	23	26	20	5	26	15	23	22	1	2	1	1	3		Apps
	6		1		2	15	9	2	5	3	8	8	1			3				3	1	1	Subs
	2		2		12	3		16	1	7	8	3		1	2	1					4		Goals

57

Crusaders FC
2004-2005 Season Statistics

1	Sep	25	A	Coleraine	D	1-1	McBride 76'
2	Oct	2	H	Dungannon Swifts	L	0-3	
3		9	A	Larne	L	2-5	Russell 47', Arthur 63' (pen)
4		16	H	Loughgall	W	3-2	Morrow 15', Russell 47', Spiers 59'
5		23	H	Ards	L	0-2	
6		30	A	Ballymena United	D	1-1	Russell 38'
7	Nov	6	A	Linfield	L	1-2	Magill 66'
8		13	H	Lisburn Distillery	D	0-0	
9		20	H	Portadown	L	0-1	
10		27	A	Omagh Town	W	3-1	Morrow 19', Russell 31', Magill 87'
11	Dec	4	A	Limavady United	D	1-1	Neill 26'
12		11	H	Newry City	L	0-1	
13		18	A	Glentoran	L	1-4	Morrow 26'
14		27	H	Cliftonville	L	0-2	
15	Jan	3	H	Coleraine	D	1-1	Spiers 47'
16		8	A	Dungannon Swifts	D	0-0	
17		22	H	Larne	D	1-1	Magill 90'
18		25	A	Institute	L	0-2	
19		29	A	Loughgall	L	0-2	
20	Feb	5	A	Ards	D	2-2	Dunne 21', Stirling 90'
21		19	H	Ballymena United	L	2-3	Stirling 25', Morrow 87'
22		26	H	Linfield	L	1-2	McDowell 9'
23	Mar	12	A	Lisburn Distillery	L	2-3	Magill 4', Armstrong 80'
24		19	A	Portadown	D	0-0	
25		24	H	Omagh Town	W	3-1	Stirling 2' 10', Livingstone 20'
26		29	H	Limavady United	W	1-0	Cooley 16' (og)
27	Apr	9	A	Newry City	L	0-2	
28		16	H	Institute	W	1-0	Stirling 51'
29		23	A	Cliftonville	L	0-1	
30		30	H	Glentoran	L	0-2	

Final League Position: 15th in the Irish Premier League

Appearances

Sub. Appearances

Goals

N. Armstrong	J. Shaw	S. McBride	L. Dunne	J. Spiers	C. Coates	P. Dickson	C. Morrow	C. Magill	B. Russell	G. Arthur	D. Munster	D. Stirling	L. Hogan	J. Braniff	S. Livingstone	A. Neill	L. Windrum	D. Magowan	I. McCoosh	A. McKee	D. Armstrong	P. Conlon	S. McClean	J. Montgomery	W. Stewart	K. McDowell	
1	2	3	4	5	6	7	8	9*	10†	11	12*	14†															1
1	2	3	4		6	5*	8	9	10†	11	7	12*	14†														2
1	2	7	4*		3	12*	8	9	10	11	14†			5†	6												3
1	2	3	4	5	6		8	9*	10†	11	12*				7	14†											4
	2†	3	4	5	6*	12*	8	9	10	11°	7					15°	1	14†									5
	2	3	4		5		8	9*	10	11	7				6	12*	1										6
	2	3	4	5	6†	12*	8	9	10	11*	7				14†		1										7
1		3	4	5			8	9			7				6	10*		2	11	12*							8
1		3	4	5			8	9*	10		7				6			2	11	12*							9
1		3	4	5			8	9†	10		7				6	14†		2	11*	12*							10
1		3	4	5	6	9	8			11†	7				14†	10*		2		12*							11
1	12*	3	4°	5†	6	9*	8			11	7				14†	10		2		15°							12
1	10†	3	4†		6	12*	8	9		11*	7				5	14†		2		15°							13
1	2	3*	4†	5	12*		8°	9	10	14†	7					15°		6	11								14
1	2	3	4	5			8†	9	10		7							6	14†	11*	12*						15
1	2	3	4	5			8		10		7					12*		11		9*			6†	14†			16
1	2	3	4	5			8	9	10		7							6		12*			11*				17
1		3	4	5			8	9	14†		7*	10°						2		12*			11†	15°	6		18
1		3	7	5			8	9				12*			4			2		10			11		6*		19
1	2	3	11	5			8		10		9				4			6		12*					7*		20
1	2	3	11°	5*	12*		8	15°	10		7	9			4			6†							14†		21
1		6		3					10		7	9			4†	12*		2			5			14†	8	11*	22
1	2	11	14†	5	3		8	9*	10		7†	12*			6						4						23
1	2	9	4	5	3†		8		10		7	12*			6						14†					11*	24
1	2	3	4	5			8				7	9†			6	14†					10		12*			11*	25
1	2	3	4	5	6		8		10			9*			7	12*										11	26
1	2	11	4	5	3†		8		10°		7				6	15°		14†			9*		12*				27
1	2	3	4	5	6		8				7	9				12*					10					11*	28
1	2	3		5			8		14†		7	9			6	4*		12*			10					11†	29
1	14†	3	4*	5	2		8		10		7	9			6†	°		15°			12*					11°	30
27	21	30	27	24	18	6	27	17	21	10	24	9		1	18	4	3	15	3	2	8		4		4	7	Apps
	2		1		2	4		1	2	1		3	5	1	3	12		4		7	5		1	5	1		Subs
		1	1	2			4	4	4	1		5			1	1					1					1	Goals

Dungannon Swifts FC
2004-2005 Season Statistics

1	Sep	25	H	Linfield	D	1-1	McAree 47'
2	Oct	2	A	Crusaders	W	3-0	Forker 11', Scullion 42', McCabe 56'
3		9	H	Ballymena United	L	1-2	Bownes 70'
4		16	A	Lisburn Distillery	L	0-2	
5		23	A	Coleraine	L	2-4	McAree 12', Walker 68'
6		29	H	Loughgall	W	1-0	Scullion 37'
7	Nov	5	A	Institute	L	2-3	Bownes 24', McAree 31' (pen)
8		13	H	Cliftonville	W	3-1	McAree 3' (pen), Adamson 41', Bownes 77'
9		20	A	Larne	L	2-3	McAree 4', Adamson 49'
10		26	H	Newry City	W	1-0	Scullion 21'
11	Dec	4	A	Glentoran	L	0-5	
12		11	A	Limavady United	L	2-3	Adamson 6', Bownes 77'
13		18	H	Portadown	L	1-3	Adamson 35'
14		27	A	Omagh Town	W	4-1	Gallagher 16', Adamson 27' 90', Walker 37'
15	Jan	1	H	Ards	W	7-0	Shaw 1' 15', Adamson 32', Bownes 42', Scullion 62', McCabe 67', Walker 80'
16		3	A	Linfield	L	1-2	Slater 76'
17		8	H	Crusaders	D	0-0	
18		22	A	Ballymena United	W	2-1	G. Fitzpatrick 40', Bownes 53'
19		29	H	Lisburn Distillery	D	1-1	Adamson 30'
20	Feb	5	H	Coleraine	L	0-1	
21		18	A	Loughgall	W	2-1	Everaldo 15', Adamson 34'
22		25	H	Institute	W	3-0	Coney 25', Bownes 76' 90'
23	Mar	12	A	Cliftonville	D	1-1	G. Fitzpatrick 85'
24		19	H	Larne	W	3-1	Bownes 13', Everaldo 68', Coney 90'
25		24	A	Newry City	W	4-0	Bownes 26' 50', McLaughlin 56', Adamson 73'
26		29	H	Glentoran	W	2-1	Scullion 49', Shaw 56'
27	Apr	9	H	Limavady United	D	1-1	Everaldo 30'
28		16	A	Ards	W	3-1	Forker 27' 87', Shaw 40'
29		23	H	Omagh Town	W	2-1	C. Mullan 72' (og), Bownes 87'
30		30	A	Portadown	W	2-1	Bownes 18' (pen), G. Fitzpatrick 76'

Final League Position: 4th in the Irish Premier League

Appearances

Sub. Appearances

Goals

	S. Addis	T. Heffernan	J. Gallagher	J. Montgomery	G. Fitzpatrick	A. Hamilton	S. McCabe	R. McAree	S. Coney	G. Bownes	S. Walker	C. Forker	T. Fitzpatrick	S. Donnelly	D. McNamee	M. Gracey	D. Scullion	K. Rafferty	P. Forker	K. McCleery	T. Adamson	A. McMinn	J. Slater	S. Shaw	P. Carville	S. Fanthorpe	R. McLaughlin	Everaldo	D. Geti	G. McKinstry	A. McCaffrey	G. Cushley	K. Camlin	
1	1	2†	3	4	5	6	7	8	9°	10*	11	12*	14†	15°																					1
2	1		3	4		6	7	8		10		9	12*		2	5	11*																		2
3	1			4	5	6*	7†	8	15°	10	12*	9°	14†		2	3	11																		3
4	1				5	6	7*	8	14†	10	9†	12*	15°		2	3°	11	4																	4
5	1		3		5	6†	14†	8		10	9	12*			2		11	4	7*																5
6	1		3	2	5	6	12*	8		10	9	7*					11	4																	6
7	1		3		5	6*	7		9†	10		14†	12*		2°		11	4		15°															7
8	1		3		5	12*	7	8°	14†	10	6*		15°		2		11	4			9†														8
9	1		3		5	12*	7		14†	10†	6*				2		11	4			9														9
10	1		3		5	6	7	8		12*	10		2				11	4			9*														10
11	1		3		5	6*	7	8			10	12*	2				11	4			9														11
12	1		7		5	6*	14†	8		12*	10		2			3†	11	4			9														12
13	1	2	3		5	6	7	8*		12*	10						11	4			9														13
14	1	2	3			12*	7	8		10*		6					11†	4			9		5	14†											14
15	1	2	3		5		7	8†		12*	14†	6					11	4			9*		15°	10°											15
16	1		3		5	15°	7	8		10	12*				2°		11	4					14†	9†	6*										16
17	1	2*	3		5		7	8		14†	10		6				11†	4					12*	9											17
18	1	2	3		5		7	8*		10	12*		6				11	4					9												18
19	1	2	6		5		7		12*	10†	8		3				11	4*			9		14†												19
20	1	2°	3		5	8	7		14†	10		12*	6†				11				9*				4	15°									20
21	1		3		5		7	8		10*							11				9	4		12*	2	6									21
22	1		3		5		7	8	9†	15°		12*					11°				4			10*	14†	2	6								22
23	1				5	6	7		9†	14†	3						11				4			8°	12*	2*	10	15°							23
24	1		3		5	2	7		15°	10			6*				12*				9°			8†	4	14†	11								24
25	1		3		5	6			14†	10		12*					11°	4		9†				8	2*	7	15°								25
26	1		3		5	6	14†		10†								11	4		9*				8	2	7	12*								26
27	1		3		5	6*	7	9			14†						11							8	4	2†	10	12*							27
28	1		3		5	6			9†	7							11*							8	4	2	10		12*	14†					28
29	1		3		5	6†			12*	10	9*	7					14†				15°			8	4	2°	11								29
30			3		5				11*	10		9	7		14†						12*			8°	4	2†						1	15°		30
	29	8	27	4	28	20	22	20	6	19	13	6	13	1	8	4	26	16	1		15	6		12	1	6	9	9			1			
						4	4		9	7	4	6	6		4	1	2		1		2	5	1	2	2		4		1	1	1			
			1		3		1	2	5	2	13	3	3				5					10		1	4				1	3				

61

Glentoran FC
2004-2005 Season Statistics

#	Month	Date	H/A	Opponent	Result	Score	Scorers
1	Sep	25	H	Portadown	L	1-2	Lockhart 41'
2	Oct	2	A	Limavady United	D	2-2	Halliday 8', Lockhart 26'
3		9	H	Lisburn Distillery	W	1-0	Holmes 19'
4		16	A	Ards	W	3-0	Lockhart 43', Morgan 55', Halliday 70'
5		23	A	Cliftonville	W	1-0	Halliday 74'
6		30	H	Coleraine	W	1-0	Nixon 50' (pen)
7	Nov	6	A	Loughgall	W	3-1	Morgan 55' 87', McLaughlin 77'
8		13	H	Institute	W	2-0	Morgan 7', Holmes 12'
9		20	A	Newry City	W	4-0	Halliday 6' 62', Nixon 17', Larkin 60' (og)
10		27	A	Larne	W	5-0	Halliday 3' 8', Glendinning 35', Holmes 47', Morgan 70'
11	Dec	4	H	Dungannon Swifts	W	5-0	Glendinning 29', Nixon 42' (pen), Melaugh 77', Lockhart 87', McLaughlin 90'
12		11	A	Omagh Town	W	3-2	Nixon 37' (pen), Halliday 55', Melaugh 83'
13		18	H	Crusaders	W	4-1	Lockhart 13', Glendinning 47' 59', Morgan 90'
14		27	A	Linfield	D	1-1	Morgan 63'
15	Jan	3	A	Portadown	L	3-4	Halliday 11', Morgan 28', Holmes 42'
16		18	H	Ballymena United	W	4-2	Halliday 4' 68', Glendinning 46', Nixon 75'
17		22	A	Lisburn Distillery	L	1-2	Halliday 53'
18		29	H	Ards	W	2-0	Lockhart 88', Morgan 90' (pen)
19	Feb	5	H	Cliftonville	W	4-0	Morgan 37' 46' 90', Lockhart 87'
20		19	A	Coleraine	W	1-0	Lockhart 4'
21		26	H	Loughgall	W	2-0	Halliday 48', Morgan 76'
22	Mar	8	H	Limavady United	W	2-0	Keegan 60', Morgan 90'
23		12	A	Institute	W	1-0	Glendinning 81'
24		19	H	Newry City	W	3-1	Morgan 42' 48', Parkhouse 89'
25		25	H	Larne	W	3-0	Keegan 4', Morgan 38', Halliday 82' (pen)
26		29	A	Dungannon Swifts	L	0-2	
27	Apr	9	H	Omagh Town	W	3-0	Halliday 4', McGibbon 11', Morgan 41'
28		16	A	Ballymena United	W	3-0	Nixon 45' (pen), Morgan 63', Ward 72'
29		23	H	Linfield	W	3-2	Parkhouse 25', Nixon 53', Morgan 90'
30		30	A	Crusaders	W	2-0	Lockhart 11', McCallion 49'

Final League Position: Champions of the Irish Premier League

Appearances

Sub. Appearances

Goals

E. Morris	C. Nixon	M. Glendinning	S. Holmes	P. Leeman	P. McGibbon	C. Morgan	T. McCallion	D. McLaughlin	M. Halliday	D. Lockhart	K. Keegan	G. Melaugh	A. Kilmartin	T. McCann	J. Mulgrew	S. Ward	C. Walker	S. Parkhouse	
1	2	3	4	5	6	7†	8°	9	10*	11	12*	14†	15°						1
1	2	3	4	5	6	7	8°	9	10*	11†	14†	12*	15°						2
1	2	3	6	5		9			10	11	8	4	7						3
1	2	3	6	5		9*		14†	10	11	8†	4	7	12*					4
1	2	3	6	5		9*		12*	10	11	8†	4	7	14†					5
1	2	3	6	5		9		12*	10*	11	8	4	7†	14†					6
1	2	3	6	5		9		12*	10†	11	8	4	7*	14†					7
1	2	3	6	5	14†	9*		12*	10†	11	8	4		7					8
1	2	3	6	5		9		12*	10†	11	8*	4		7	14†				9
1	2	3	6†	5		9*		12*	10	11	8	4	14†	7					10
1	2	3	6†	5		9*		12*	10	11	8	7		14†		4			11
1	2	3	6	5		9*		12*	10	11	8†	7	14†			4			12
1	2	3	6	5		9			10	11	8*	7	12*			4			13
1	2	3	6	5		9*	14†	12*	10	11	8†	7				4			14
1	2	3	6	5		9*	8	12*	10	11		7				4			15
1	2	3	6	5		9	8*		10	11	12*	7				4			16
1	2	3	6†	5		9		12*	10	11	8*	7	14†			4			17
1		3		5	6	9	14†		10*	11	8†	7				2	4	12*	18
1		3	6†	5		9	14†	12*		11		7		8		2	4	10*	19
1		3		5		9			10*	11	8	7	14†	6		2	4†	12*	20
1		3		5	4	9			10	11	8*	7		6		2		12*	21
1		3	12*	5	4	9			10	11*	8	7		6		2			22
1		3	11	5	4	9			10		8*	7		6		2		12*	23
1		3	11†	5	4	9	15°		10*		8°	7		6		2	14†	12*	24
1		3	12*	5	6*	9	14†		10		8	7		11†		2	4		25
1	2	3	14†	5	15°	9			10†		8°	7		11*		6	4	12*	26
1	2	3	14†	5†	6	9	15°		10*			7		11°		8	4	12*	27
1	2	3		5*	6	9	12*		10	11						8	4		28
1	2	3		5	4	9			10		12*	7		11*		8		6	29
1	2	3		5	4	9*	8		10	11		7				12*		6	30
30	22	28	22	29	13	30	5	2	29	23	21	28	5	14		19	7	3	Apps
			4		2		7	12	1		4	2	6	6	1	1	1	7	Subs
	7	6	4		1	20	1	2	15	9	2	2				1		2	Goals

Institute FC
2004-2005 Season Statistics

#	Month	Date	H/A	Opponent	Result	Score	Scorers
1	Sep	25	H	Ards	D	1-1	Paul McLaughlin 73'
2	Oct	2	A	Linfield	L	1-3	I. Sproule 90'
3		9	H	Portadown	W	2-1	Ogilby 15' (pen), Paul McLaughlin 78'
4		16	A	Ballymena United	D	1-1	Paul McLaughlin 24'
5		22	H	Newry City	W	2-1	Ogilby 68', Mooney 84'
6		30	A	Larne	L	0-2	
7	Nov	5	H	Dungannon Swifts	W	3-2	Philson 32', I. Sproule 63', G. Sproule 68'
8		13	A	Glentoran	L	0-2	
9		20	H	Coleraine	W	3-1	Coyle 32', G. Sproule 72' 90'
10		26	A	Cliftonville	L	0-1	
11	Dec	4	A	Loughgall	W	1-0	Divin 47'
12		11	H	Lisburn Distillery	L	1-3	Ogilby 50' (pen)
13		17	H	Omagh Town	L	0-1	
14		27	A	Limavady United	L	1-5	Coyle 4'
15	Jan	22	A	Portadown	L	0-4	
16		25	H	Crusaders	W	2-0	G. Sproule 5', Stewart 42' (og)
17		29	H	Ballymena United	D	1-1	Whitehead 24'
18	Feb	1	A	Ards	W	2-1	Porter 13', Whitehead 55'
19		4	A	Newry City	L	1-4	Wray 66'
20		19	H	Larne	W	3-0	Whitehead 61' (pen), G. Sproule 70', Mooney 81'
21		25	A	Dungannon Swifts	L	0-3	
22	Mar	5	H	Linfield	L	0-1	
23		12	H	Glentoran	L	0-1	
24		19	A	Coleraine	W	4-2	Mooney 26', G. Sproule 43' 90', Whitehead 72'
25		24	H	Cliftonville	L	1-2	Semple 19'
26		29	H	Loughgall	W	3-0	Whitehead 14', Paul McLaughlin 54', Wray 69'
27	Apr	9	A	Lisburn Distillery	L	2-3	Whitehead 18', Mooney 72'
28		16	A	Crusaders	L	0-1	
29		22	H	Limavady United	L	0-3	
30		30	A	Omagh Town	W	1-0	Blair 61'

Final League Position: 9th in the Irish Premier League

Appearances

Sub. Appearances

Goals

C. McLaughlin	G. Philson	R. Dunlop	J. McElroy	P. Hegarty	J. Quigley	R. Semple	G. Doherty	S. Bratton	R. Coyle	D. Divin	M. McCann	Paul McLaughlin	D. Nash	D. Ogilby	I. Sproule	T. Wray	G. Sproule	J. Curran	G. Crossan	C. Mooney	S. McCabe	T. Gray	R. Porter	D. Whitehead	Paddy McLaughlin	A. Blair	A. Ryan	M. Smith	M. O'Hagan	P. Kelly	K. McWilliams	B. Devine	
1	2	3	4	5°	6	7*	8†	9	10	11	12*	14†	15°																				1
1	2	3	4	10†	6*			9	12*	11	8	14†		5	7																		2
1	2	3		6†		7	9*		14†	11	8	12*		4	10	5																	3
1	2	3		5		7			12*	11	8	9		4	10	6	14†	15°															4
	2	3			6	7			14†	11†	8	9*		4	10	5			1	12*													5
		3†		6°	7			9	12*	11	8	10*		4	5			15°	1	14†	2												6
	2	3					6	12*	9	11	8			10†	5*	7			1	14†	4												7
	2	3		6†		12*			10	11*	8	14†		5	7	9			1				4										8
	2			6*		7			10	12*	8			4	11	5	9		1				3										9
	2		6†*	12*	7				10	14†	8	15°		4	11	5	9°		1				3										10
	2	3		6		7			10	11	8	12*		4	9*	5			1														11
	2	3*		6		7	14†		10†	11	8	12*		4	9	5			1														12
1	2	3		6*		7			10	11*	8	12*		4	9	5		14†															13
	2	3	14†			7†	11		10	15°	8	12*		4		5	9*	6°	1														14
1	2	3°			7†	8*	12*	10	11			14†	15°			9	6				5		4										15
1	2	12*				10	15°		11†					4		5	8	7		6*		3	14†	9°									16
1	2	12*				9†	14†							6		5	8	7		10*		3	4	11									17
1	2	12*				14†	11*							6		5	8	7		10		3	4	9†									18
1	2	3*				9†								6		5	8	7		10	12*		11		4	14†							19
	2								11		10		6*		5	8	7†		15°	4	3	14†	9°		12*	1							20
	2	12*							11				6		5	8			14†	7	3	4	9†		10*	1							21
2†					7°	10			11					4		5	8	6		12*		14†	9*	3	15°	1							22
1					7	10†			11					4		5	8	6		14†	12*	2	9*	3									23
					7				11		9†			4		5	8	6		10*	2	12*	14†	3		1							24
1		12*			7	14†			11		15°	3*		4		5	8	6†		10°				9	2								25
					7			10	11		6†			4		5	8*			14†			9	2	12*	1	3						26
					7†			10	11					4		5				8		12*	9	2	6*	1	3	14†					27
	2				7			10	11		12*			4		5				8*		6	9	3		1							28
	2				7				11		14†			4		5	8			6*				12*	3		1	15°		9°	10†		29
	2								11°		12*	10†		4	5	8					6		9*		14†	1	3	15°				7	30
12	24	14	2	10	5	20	9	5	12	24	13	6	2	27	11	26	19	11	9	9	6	9	7	12	9	2	9	3		1	1	1	
	5	1		1	3	2	3	5	3	1	3	2	1	11	26	1	3		8	2		5	2		5		1	2					
		1			1			2	1		4		3	2	2	7		4			1	6		1									

Larne FC
2004-2005 Season Statistics

1	Sep	25	H	Omagh Town	W	2-0	Dickson 2' 39' (pen)
2	Oct	2	A	Portadown	L	0-3	
3		9	H	Crusaders	W	5-2	McKnight 14', Weir 22', Dickson 32', Loverso 44', Parker 73'
4		16	A	Limavady United	L	0-6	
5		23	A	Loughgall	W	2-0	Dickson 22' 50' (pen)
6		30	H	Institute	W	2-0	Murphy 31', Curran 85'
7	Nov	5	H	Newry City	L	0-1	
8		12	A	Coleraine	L	0-3	
9		20	H	Dungannon Swifts	W	3-2	Parker 18', Okaniya 53', Dickson 90'
10		27	H	Glentoran	L	0-5	
11	Dec	4	A	Cliftonville	L	0-2	
12		11	A	Linfield	D	1-1	Wray 7'
13		18	H	Ballymena United	D	0-0	
14		27	A	Ards	W	3-0	Curran 16', Weir 76', Dickson 79'
15	Jan	3	A	Omagh Town	L	0-3	
16		8	H	Portadown	L	2-3	Rodgers 19', Dickson 39'
17		22	A	Crusaders	D	1-1	Dickson 88'
18		25	H	Lisburn Distillery	D	0-0	
19		29	H	Limavady United	L	0-4	
20	Feb	5	H	Loughgall	L	2-3	Hamlin 5', Ogden 54'
21		19	A	Institute	L	0-3	
22		25	A	Newry City	W	3-1	Murphy 13', Dickson 20' (pen) 58'
23	Mar	11	H	Coleraine	L	1-5	Dickson 82' (pen)
24		19	A	Dungannon Swifts	L	1-3	Dickson 45' (pen)
25		25	A	Glentoran	L	0-3	
26		28	H	Cliftonville	D	0-0	
27	Apr	9	H	Linfield	L	0-2	
28		16	A	Lisburn Distillery	L	1-2	Murphy 45'
29		23	H	Ards	D	2-2	Dickson 29' (pen) 62' (pen)
30		30	A	Ballymena United	D	0-0	

Final League Position: 13th in the Irish Premier League

Appearances

Sub. Appearances

Goals

C. Keenan	S. Small	J. Hughes	P. Curran	A. Murphy	R. Weir	G. Wray	M. Rodgers	B. Tumilty	M. Dickson	S. Loverso	W. Lorrimer	A. McKnight	J. Crossley	O. Okunaiya	M. Parker	R. Kane	D. Kernohan	A. Spackman	N. Ogden	R. Black	A. Bonner	L. Hamlin	A. McCullough	D. Gordon	W. Wharry	A. Hamilton	F. Wilson	F. Small	B. McGonigle	J. McGreevy	
1	2	3	4	5	6°	7	8*	9	10	11†	12*	14†	15°																		1
1	2	3	4		6°	5	8*	9†	10	11	12*	7	14†	15°																	2
1		3°	4	5	8†	2	7		10	11*	12*	9	15°					6	14†												3
1	14†	3	4	5*	8	2	7†		10	11	12*	9°	15°					6													4
1	3	5	4			2	7°		10	11*	14†	9†	12*					6	8	15°											5
1	8°	3	4	5	9†	2	7*		10				12*		11			6	14†												6
1		3	4	5		2	7	8	10	14†					11*	12*		6	9†												7
		3	4°	5		2	8	9	10						11*	14†		6	7†	1	12*	15°									8
		3	4	5	8*	2	7	9†	10				15°			14†		6	12*	1	11°										9
		3	4	5	8	2	7		10						9*			6	1	11	12*										10
	2	3	4	5	7*	8			10	14†	11†	12*						6	1		9										11
	2	3	4	5	7	8†			10	12*	11	14†						6	1		9*										12
	2	3	4	5	7	9*	8		10	14†	11†	12*						6	1												13
	2	3	4†	5	8	7°	9	11	10	15°	14†	12*						6*	1												14
	2	3	4	5	8	7°	9†	11	10	15°	14†	12*						6*	1												15
	2	3	4	5		7°	8		10	14†	11†	12*						6*	1		9	15°									16
12*		4	5	11†		7*	8	10			3	14†						6	1	15°	2	9°									17
1		4	5	12*	2		6	10		3	9°				15°			8*	14†	7		11†									18
1		3	4*	5	7	2		8	10		11							12*		6	9										19
	2	3		5	11*	4†	8		10	12*								1	7		6	9			14†						20
	2	3	4	5	8†		11		10	14†					12*			1	7°		6*	9					15°				21
	2	6	4*	5	14†		12*		10	9°					7	15°		1	3†		8	11									22
		9		5	12*	2°	7		10	11*					6	15°		1	14†		8				4	3†					23
1		6	4	5	9		3†		10	12*	11	7°	14†			8*		2				15°									24
1		3	4	5		2	14†		10	9°		7	15°		6†			8*	11								12*				25
	2*	3	4	5	6	7°			10	14†	15°	11†	12*		1			8	9												26
	2	3		5	8	4	14†	12*	10	9		7			1†	6*					11					14†					27
	2	3		5	8*	4		9	10	10†	12*	7				6°				15°	11						14†				28
1	2	5	4		8		7*	10		11†		12*				6	9							3			14†				29
12*					3	8°				11	9°	6	14†		1*			2			4			7	10	5	15°				30
13	19	29	21	26	18	22	21	17	28	5		8	13	3	23	3		17	11	1	13	11		1	2	2	1	1	1		Apps
1	2			3			3	1		5	6	5	15	8	3	10	1		3	4	1		1		2	1	2	1		1	Subs
		2	3	2	1	1				15	1		1		1	2			1		1										Goals

67

Limavady United FC
2004-2005 Season Statistics

1	Sep	25	A	Newry City	D	2-2	Brown 34' 54'
2	Oct	2	H	Glentoran	D	2-2	K. Ramsey 65', Sweeney 90'
3		9	A	Loughgall	D	1-1	K. Ramsey 25'
4		16	H	Larne	W	6-0	Brown 6' 67', K. Ramsey 14' 55', Collier 28', McDaid 77'
5		23	H	Lisburn Distillery	D	2-2	McKeown 27' (og), McCallum 85'
6		30	A	Omagh Town	W	5-2	Brown 9' 18' 37', Sweeney 54' (pen), K. Ramsey 60'
7	Nov	6	H	Ards	L	0-1	
8		13	A	Portadown	W	1-0	Sweeney 87'
9		20	H	Ballymena United	W	2-1	McCallum 60', K. Ramsey 81'
10		27	A	Linfield	L	1-4	Brown 60'
11	Dec	4	H	Crusaders	D	1-1	Sweeney 13'
12		11	H	Dungannon Swifts	W	3-2	Brown 33', K. Ramsey 62', McIlmoyle 88'
13		17	A	Coleraine	W	2-1	Sweeney 21', Brown 42'
14		27	H	Institute	W	5-1	K. Ramsey 37' 47', Brown 65', Owens 73', Callaghan 90'
15	Jan	3	H	Newry City	W	3-2	K. Ramsey 43' 70', Owens 63'
16		22	H	Loughgall	D	1-1	K. Ramsey 17'
17		29	A	Larne	W	4-0	K. Ramsey 10', Brown 18', Sweeney 45', Callaghan 90'
18	Feb	5	A	Lisburn Distillery	D	1-1	K. Ramsey 49'
19		19	H	Omagh Town	W	2-0	Patrick 16', Sweeney 64' (pen)
20		26	A	Ards	W	1-0	K. Ramsey 45'
21	Mar	2	A	Cliftonville	W	2-0	Devanney 3', McIlmoyle 53'
22		8	A	Glentoran	L	0-2	
23		12	H	Portadown	L	0-2	
24		19	A	Ballymena United	L	1-2	K. Ramsey 6'
25		23	H	Linfield	L	0-1	
26		29	A	Crusaders	L	0-1	
27	Apr	9	A	Dungannon Swifts	D	1-1	K. Ramsey 43' (pen)
28		16	H	Cliftonville	D	0-0	
29		22	A	Institute	W	3-0	Sweeney 13' (pen), K. Ramsey 43', Brown 85'
30		30	H	Coleraine	L	0-3	

Final League Position: 5th in the Irish Premier League

Appearances

Sub. Appearances

Goals

G. Ramsey	M. Watson	S. Collier	L. Patrick	L. Cooley	S. McCallum	M. McDaid	V. Sweeney	K. Ramsey	P. Brown	R. McIlmoyle	D. Patton	M. Cutmore	C. Logue	A. Callaghan	B. Devenney	D. Bulow	C. Lynch	N. Mullan	J. McDonald	M. Doherty	P. Owens	R. Stewart	
1	2	3	4	5	6	7	8	9*	10	11	12*												1
1		2	4	5	6	7°	8	9†	10	11	12*	3*	14†	15°									2
1		2	4	5	6	7	12°*	9†	10	11		3		15°	8*	14†							3
1		2	4*	5	6	7†		9	10	11		3		14†	8	15°	12*						4
1		2	4	5	6	7*	12*	9†	10	11		3			8	14†							5
1		2†	4	5	6	12*	7	9°	10*	11		3			8	15°		14†					6
1		2	4†	5	6	7		9°	10*	11	12*	3		14†	8				15°				7
1		2	4	5	6	7†	12*	9*	10	11		3			8°		15°		14†				8
1			4	5	6	7*	12*	9°	10	11		3		2	8†		14†		15°				9
1		2	4	5*	6		7†	9°	10	11		3		12*	8	15°	14†						10
		2	4		6°	7		9†	10*	11		3		5	8		12*		14†	1	15°		11
		2	4	5	6		7	9*	10	11		3			8		12*			1			12
		2	4	5	6		7	9*	10			3			8		12*			1	11		13
		2		5	6		7	9°	10			3		14†	8*	15°	4		12*	1	11†		14
		2	4	5	6		7	9†	10	15°		3			8*		12*		14†	1	11°		15
		2	4	5	6		7	9	10	11		3			8*		12*			1			16
			4	5		7*		9°	10	11†		3		2	12*		8	6	15°	1	14†		17
			4	5	6		7	9†	10	11		3		2	12*		8*		14†	1			18
		2	4	5	6		7	9*		11		3		10	8				12*	1			19
		2	4	5	6		10*	9°	12*	11†		3		7			8		15°	1	14†		20
			4	5	6		7	9†	10	11		3	12*	2	8*				14†	1			21
		2	4°	5	6		7	9	10	11*		3		14†	8†		12*		15°	1			22
		2	4	5	6	12*	7	9	10*			3			8					1	11		23
	12*		4	5	6		7†	9	10			3*		2			8			1	11	14†	24
			4	5	6	7	10	9		14†		3		2	8*				12*	1	11†		25
			4	5°	6	7*	10	9†		11		3		2			8	14†		1	12*	15°	26
		2	4	5		7		9*		11		3		8				6	10†	1	12*	14†	27
		2	4	5		7*		9†	14†	11		3		8			12*	6	10	1			28
		2†	4	5		15°	7°	9*	10	11		3		8			14†	6	12*	1			29
		2	4°	5		12*	7†	9*	10	11		3		8			15°	6	14†	1			30
10	1	23	29	29	25	12	22	30	24	24		29		14	19		6	5	2	20	6		Apps
	1					4	4		2	2	3		2	7	2	6	11	2	17		5	3	Subs
		1	1		2	1	8	18	13	2				2	1						2		Goals

Linfield FC
2004-2005 Season Statistics

1	Sep	25	A	Dungannon Swifts	D	1-1	O'Kane 19' (pen)
2	Oct	2	H	Institute	W	3-1	Ogilby 8' (og), Gault 44', Ferguson 81'
3		9	A	Newry City	W	3-0	Crawford 57', Ferguson 65', W. Murphy 77'
4		16	H	Coleraine	W	4-1	O'Kane 23' 57' (pen), Hunter 43', Gault 83'
5		23	H	Ballymena United	L	0-1	
6		30	A	Ards	D	2-2	O'Kane 18', Larmour 22'
7	Nov	6	H	Crusaders	W	2-1	Douglas 28', Hunter 35'
8		13	A	Omagh Town	W	8-1	Hunter 50' 69', Thompson 53', Larmour 55', D. Murphy 60', King 66', O'Kane 78', Picking 90'
9		20	H	Lisburn Distillery	W	5-2	Thompson 11' 63', Hunter 75', Picking 77', Larmour 82'
10		27	H	Limavady United	W	4-1	Thompson 8' 11', G. Ramsey 25' (og), Crawford 81'
11	Dec	4	A	Portadown	W	1-0	Thompson 64'
12		11	H	Larne	D	1-1	Larmour 83'
13		18	A	Cliftonville	D	0-0	
14		27	H	Glentoran	D	1-1	McAreavey 37'
15	Jan	1	A	Loughgall	W	4-0	Thompson 50' 65' 82', King 90'
16		3	H	Dungannon Swifts	W	2-1	Hunter 28', Thompson 65'
17		22	H	Newry City	W	2-0	Gault 21', Campbell 73'
18		29	A	Coleraine	W	4-0	Thompson 49', Ferguson 50', McAreavey 59', Picking 76'
19	Feb	5	A	Ballymena United	W	4-3	Thompson 17' 25', Ferguson 60', Hunter 64' (pen)
20		19	H	Ards	W	3-0	Mouncey 34', Ferguson 47', O'Kane 69'
21		26	A	Crusaders	W	2-1	O'Kane 30' 85'
22	Mar	5	A	Institute	W	1-0	Ryan 13' (og)
23		12	H	Omagh Town	W	6-1	Ferguson 18' 63' 67', Thompson 20', Larmour 83' 89'
24		19	A	Lisburn Distillery	W	4-0	Larmour 15' 65' 90', Ferguson 57'
25		23	A	Limavady United	W	1-0	Ferguson 25' (pen)
26		29	H	Portadown	D	0-0	
27	Apr	9	A	Larne	W	2-0	Douglas 28', McAreavey 59'
28		16	H	Loughgall	W	3-0	King 43', Percy 44' (og), Douglas 84'
29		23	A	Glentoran	L	2-3	McAreavey 34', Larmour 84'
30		30	H	Cliftonville	W	3-1	Picking 47', Ferguson 69' (pen), O'Kane 89'

Final League Position: 2nd in the Irish Premier League

Appearances

Sub. Appearances

Goals

A. Mannus	S. Douglas	D. Murphy	A. O'Kane	W. Murphy	M. Gault	P. Thompson	F. Simpson	G. Ferguson	M. Picking	N. Bailie	P. McAreavey	S. King	A. Crawford	P. Charnock	P. McShane	D. Larmour	A. Hunter	B. Spence	G. Dunlop	R. McCann	S. Campbell	J. Ervin	T. Mouncey	
1	2	3	4*	5	6	7	8†	9°	10	11	12*	14†	15°											1
1	2	3	4*	5	6	7	8†	9	15°	11		14†	10°	12*										2
1	2	3	4	5	6	7		9*	15°	11†		14†	10°		8	12*								3
1	2	3	4	5*	6	7	8†	9	15°			14†	10°		12*		11							4
1	2	3	4		6	7	8*		10			12*	14†	5		9	11†							5
1	2	5	4†		6°	7	15°		12*			14†	10*	8	3	9	11							6
1	2	5	4*		6	7	14†		10			12*	15°	8†	3	9°	11							7
1	2	10†	4		6	12*		8		11°		14†	7*		3	9	5	15°						8
1	2*	10	4†		6	7		8		11		12*			3	9	5		14†					9
1	2	10†	4°		6	7		8		11		14†	12*		3*	9	5		15°					10
1	2	10	4		6	7		8*		11		12*			3	9	5							11
1	2*	10	4†		6	7		8		11		15°	12*		3	9	5°		14†					12
1	2°	10*	4		6	7		8		11		12*	14†		3	9†					15°			13
1	2	10	12*			7		9	8	11		4*	3				5			6				14
1	2	10	15°		12*	7		9†	8	11		4°	3			14†	5			6*				15
1	2*	10†	14†		12*	7		9	8	11		4	3				5			6				16
1	2	10			8	7°		9	3*	11		4†	12*		14†		5			6	15°			17
1		10	14†		8	7		9°	3	11		4†	12*				5			6*	15°	2		18
1		10	14†		8	7°		9	3	11		4	12*				5			6†	15°	2*		19
1	2	10	12*		8			9†	15°	11		4°			14†		5*			6	7		3	20
1		10	6		8	7		9	4	11		12*					5	2*					3	21
1	2		6	5	8†	7		9*	4°	11		10			12*					3	15°	14†		22
1	2	10	6†	5	8°	7		9	4*	11		14†			12*				15°	3				23
1	2	10		5	8	7		9		11		12*			6	4				3*				24
1	2			5	8	7		9		11		10			6	4				3				25
1	2	12*		5	8	7		9	14†	11		10			6	4†				3*				26
1	2	6†	15°	5	8°	7		9	12*	11		10			3	4*				14†				27
1	2	6		5	8°	12*		9*	7†	11		10	3			4				15°	14†			28
1	2	4†	15°	5		7		9	12*	11		10	3			14†				6	8*			29
1	2	4	12*	5		7		9	8	11		10†	3*							6°	14†		15°	30
30	27	26	17	13	25	27	4	21	20	26		13	7	5	3	13	14	18	1	14	2	2	2	Apps
	1	9		2	2	2		8			1	19	6	1	2	6		1	4	3	6		2	Subs
	3	1	9	1	3	14		11	4		4	3	2			10	7				1		1	Goals

Lisburn Distillery FC
2004-2005 Season Statistics

1	Sep	25	A	Cliftonville	L	0-1	
2	Oct	2	H	Coleraine	D	2-2	Willis 8', Armour 52'
3		9	A	Glentoran	L	0-1	
4		16	H	Dungannon Swifts	W	2-0	Armour 42' 47'
5		23	A	Limavady United	D	2-2	Willis 9', Armour 46'
6		30	H	Portadown	W	2-0	Armour 68', Mouncey 71'
7	Nov	6	H	Omagh Town	W	6-1	Armour 7' (pen) 74' (pen), Lyttle 31', Willis 34', Murphy 57', Anderson 90'
8		13	A	Crusaders	D	0-0	
9		20	A	Linfield	L	2-5	Buchanan 23', Murphy 30'
10		27	H	Ballymena United	L	0-2	
11	Dec	4	H	Ards	D	1-1	Mouncey 57'
12		11	A	Institute	W	3-1	Murphy 12', Armour 60', Willis 79'
13		18	A	Loughgall	L	1-2	Muir 12'
14		27	H	Newry City	L	1-3	Paul McLaughlin 59' (og)
15	Jan	3	H	Cliftonville	W	3-1	Anderson 50', Murphy 63' 90' (pen)
16		18	A	Coleraine	W	3-1	Armour 80', Murphy 82', Barron 87'
17		22	H	Glentoran	W	2-1	Martin 25', Armour 73' (pen)
18		25	A	Larne	D	0-0	
19		29	A	Dungannon Swifts	D	1-1	Willis 86'
20	Feb	5	H	Limavady United	D	1-1	Armour 56'
21		19	A	Portadown	L	1-2	Hagan 67'
22		24	A	Omagh Town	W	3-2	Dickson 35', Anderson 63', Armour 77'
23	Mar	12	H	Crusaders	W	3-2	Willis 24', Murphy 56' 87'
24		19	H	Linfield	L	0-4	
25		24	A	Ballymena United	L	1-2	Armour 44'
26		29	A	Ards	W	1-0	Martin 45'
27	Apr	9	H	Institute	W	3-2	Martin 4', Armour 25', Dickson 76'
28		16	H	Larne	W	2-1	Murphy 51' (pen), Willis 56'
29		23	A	Newry City	D	0-0	
30		30	H	Loughgall	W	3-1	Martin 37', Willis 44' 80'

Final League Position: 7th in the Irish Premier League

Appearances

Sub. Appearances

Goals

P. Matthews	P. Prenter	M. Ferguson	N. Anderson	W. Buchanan	P. Muir	C. Hagan	T. Mouncey	D. Armour	J. Willis	F. Murphy	A. Cleary	A. Dickson	G. McKeown	G. Lyttle	D. Wright	M. Dougherty	M. Holland	J. Martin	A. Barron	S. Thompson	C. Coffey	A. Johnston	
1	2°	3	4*	5	6	7†	8	9	10	11	12*	14†	15°										1
1	2	3	11	5			8	9	10*		14†	7	4	6†	12*								2
1	2*	3	7	5	6	12*	8	9	10	11			4										3
	2	3	7	5	6*		8	9	10†	11		12*	4		14†	1							4
	15°	3	8	5	6			9	10†	11		2*	4	7°		1	12*	14†					5
	12*	3	15°	5	6		8	9†	10	11		2*	4	7°		1	14†						6
		3	14†	5	6		8†	9°	10*	11		2	4	7		1	12*	15°					7
		3	14†	5	6		8	9	10*	11		2	4	7†		1	12*						8
	2		12*	5		15°	8		10†	11	3	6°	4	7*		1	9	14†					9
1	12*	3	7†	5	6		8	9	10°	11		2	4*	14†				15°					10
1	2	3	14†		6		8	9	12*	11		5	4	10†				7*					11
1		3	7	5	6	2	8*	9	14†	11			4	12*				10†					12
1		3	8*	5	6	2		9	10	11	12*	15°	4°	7†				14†					13
1		3	8	5	6	4		12*	10†	11	2	14†		7*				9					14
1	2	3	5		6	7		9*	12*	11	8†	15°	4					10°	14†				15
1		3	8*	5	6	7		9	12*	11		14†	4					10†	2				16
1		3	8	5	6	7		9*	12*	11			4					10	2				17
1	14†	3	8	5†	6	7		9	12*	11			4					10	2*				18
1	2	3	8		6*	5		9	10	11	12*		4					14†	7†				19
1	2	3	8†		6°	5		9	10	11	12*		4					7*	14†	15°			20
	2	3	8			5		9	10*			6		4	12*	1		14†	7†		11		21
		3	8		6	2		9*		11†	4	7			12*	1		10	14†		5		22
		3	8*	5	6	2			9†	11	15°	7°	4		14†	1		10			12*		23
		3	8*	5	6	2			9	11	7°	14†	4			1			15°	10†	12*		24
	12*	3		5	6	2		9°		11	7*		4			1		10	14†		8†	15°	25
		3	8		6	2		9*	12*	11			4			1		10		5	7		26
		3		5	6	4		9*	12*	11		14†				1		10	8	2	7†		27
		3		5	6	4		9°	12*	11	15°	14†				1		10†	8	2*	7		28
		3			6	5		9	10	11		12*	4			1		10	8	2	7*		29
		3			6	5		9	12*	11			4			1		10	8	2*	7		30
14	10	29	20	21	27	20	11	26	18	28	7	10	25	9		16	1	14	11	5	8		Apps
	5		5			2		1	10		7	10	1	2	5		4	4	8	4	2	1	Subs
		3	1	1	1	2	14	9	9		2		1					4	1				Goals

Loughgall FC
2004-2005 Season Statistics

1	Sep	25	H	Ballymena United	W	1-0	Wilson 87'
2	Oct	2	A	Omagh Town	W	2-1	Quilty 9' 30'
3		9	H	Limavady United	D	1-1	Emerson 55'
4		16	A	Crusaders	L	2-3	Emerson 19', Coulter 78' (pen)
5		23	H	Larne	L	0-2	
6		29	A	Dungannon Swifts	L	0-1	
7	Nov	6	H	Glentoran	L	1-3	Percy 62'
8		12	A	Newry City	W	5-2	Wilson 11', Coulter 24' 29' 43', McNally 85'
9		20	H	Cliftonville	D	0-0	
10		27	A	Coleraine	L	0-2	
11	Dec	4	H	Institute	L	0-1	
12		14	A	Ards	D	0-0	
13		18	H	Lisburn Distillery	W	2-1	Harbinson 19', Sterritt 65'
14		27	A	Portadown	D	2-2	Emerson 49', Sterritt 82'
15	Jan	1	H	Linfield	L	0-4	
16		3	A	Ballymena United	L	1-2	Emerson 19'
17		22	A	Limavady United	D	1-1	Sterritt 47'
18		29	H	Crusaders	W	2-0	Emerson 50', Sterritt 67'
19	Feb	1	H	Omagh Town	L	1-3	Coulter 12'
20		5	A	Larne	W	3-2	Sterritt 60' 81', Emerson 86'
21		18	H	Dungannon Swifts	L	1-2	Coulter 82'
22		26	A	Glentoran	L	0-2	
23	Mar	11	H	Newry City	D	1-1	Percy 63'
24		19	A	Cliftonville	W	3-1	Adair 45', N. Robinson 52', Emerson 65'
25		24	H	Coleraine	L	1-5	Sterritt 35'
26		29	A	Institute	L	0-3	
27	Apr	9	H	Ards	W	3-1	Wilson 7', Harbinson 36', Percy 59'
28		16	A	Linfield	L	0-3	
29		21	H	Portadown	L	0-3	
30		30	A	Lisburn Distillery	L	1-3	Peden 13'

Final League Position: 12th in the Irish Premier League

Appearances

Sub. Appearances

Goals

M. Robinson	G. Waddell	C. Guiney	D. Peden	N. Robinson	P. Harbinson	A. Emerson	K. Percy	S. Coulter	B. Quilty	B. Adair	A. Wilson	S. McNally	J. Guy	I. Wallace	K. Henry	C. Sterritt	S. O'Neill	W. Herron	J. Black	J. Jess	A. Beck	M. Cromie	G. Maguire	B. Pentland	
1	2	3	4	5	6	7	8	9†	10*	11	12*	14†													1
1	2	3	4	5	6	7	8	9*	10†	11	12*			14†											2
1	2	3	4	5†	6	7	8	9	10*	11		14†		12*											3
1	2*	3	4	15°	6	7	8	11	10†	5°		14†	9	12*											4
1	3		2	5	6†	7	8	10		11°	14†	15°	9*	4	12*										5
1	2	3	4	5	6	7				8	9		12*	10*	11										6
1	2		4	5*	6	7	8	9		11	10				3	12*									7
1	2	15°	4	5	6	7	8	9†		11	10*	14†			3°	12*									8
1	2†	14†	4	5	6	7	8	9	10*	11					3	12*									9
1	2†	14†	4	5	6	7*	8	9		11	10°				3†	12*	15°								10
1	2	3	4	5*	6	7†	8			11	10				12*	14†	9								11
1	2	3†	5		6	7								4	9	10*		8	11	12*	14†				12
1	2	3	9		6	7	8			5	12*			4	10*				11						13
1	2	3	9	15°	6†	7	8			5*	14†			4	12*	10*			11						14
1	2	3	9	15°	6	7	8			5*	14†			4°	12*	10			11†						15
1	2	3	4		6	7	8			11	9				10*			5	12*						16
1	2	3	4	5	6	7	8				9†				12*	10*			11	14†					17
1	2*		4	5	6	7°	8	9	15°		14†				12*	10†			11	3					18
1	2	3	4	5*	6		8	9	14†		12*					10			7	11†					19
1	2		4	14†	6	7	8	9		11*					12*	10†			5	3					20
1	2	3	4	12*	6	7	8	9	14†	11†						10			5*						21
1	2	3*	4	5	6	7°	8			14†	11				15°	10†			9	12*					22
1			4			7	8	9		5	12*		10		3	14†		6*				2	11†		23
1	2		4	5		7		9		15°	11	14†	8†	6°	10*	12*								3	24
1	2	3	4†	5		7		9		14†	12*			6	10	8								11*	25
1	2	3	4	5		7	8	9			12*			11†	6	10*	14†								26
1	2	3	4	5	6	7*	8°	9	14†	11	10†				12*	15°									27
1	2	3	4	5	6°	7	8†	9	14†	11*	10				12*	15°									28
1	2	11°	4*	5			8	9	14†	7					6	10†	12*	15°						3	29
1	2*	7	4	5	6		8	9	10°						11	15°	12*	14†						3†	30
30	29	21	30	21	25	27	26	21	6	21	11		6	8	9	15	1	9	8			1	1	4	Apps
	3		5						9			14	4	2	1	8	9	1	6	5	1	1			Subs
		1	1	2	7	3	6	2	1	3	1					7									Goals

Newry City FC
2004-2005 Season Statistics

1	Sep	25	H	Limavady United	D	2-2	Collier 27' (og), Meehan 41'
2	Oct	2	A	Ballymena United	L	1-2	Curran 39'
3		9	H	Linfield	L	0-3	
4		15	A	Omagh Town	D	2-2	Curran 21', Casey 32'
5		22	A	Institute	L	1-2	McHugh 69'
6		29	H	Cliftonville	W	4-2	McCullagh 14' 31', Meehan 77' 81'
7	Nov	5	A	Larne	W	1-0	Meehan 31'
8		12	H	Loughgall	L	2-5	Meehan 15', Casey 17' (pen)
9		20	H	Glentoran	L	0-4	
10		26	A	Cliftonville	L	0-1	
11	Dec	4	H	Coleraine	L	0-1	
12		11	A	Crusaders	W	1-0	Curran 55'
13		17	H	Ards	W	1-0	McCullagh 8'
14		27	A	Lisburn Distillery	W	3-1	Johnston 26', McHugh 37', Friel 55'
15		30	H	Portadown	L	0-6	
16	Jan	3	A	Limavady United	L	2-3	Meehan 54', McCullagh 72'
17		22	A	Linfield	L	0-2	
18		28	H	Omagh Town	W	2-1	Donohoe 79', Friel 90'
19	Feb	4	H	Institute	W	4-1	Crawford 5' 23', Farrell 17', Donohoe 90'
20		19	A	Cliftonville	W	1-0	Farrell 87'
21		25	H	Larne	L	1-3	Meehan 77'
22	Mar	1	H	Ballymena United	D	1-1	Farrell 52'
23		11	A	Loughgall	D	1-1	Clarke 42'
24		19	A	Glentoran	L	1-3	Meehan 81'
25		24	H	Dung	L	0-4	
26		29	A	Coleraine	L	1-6	McHugh 78'
27	Apr	9	H	Crusaders	W	2-0	Farrell 67', Donohoe 90'
28		16	A	Portadown	W	3-2	McLaughlin 28', Donohoe 72' 87'
29		23	H	Lisburn Distillery	D	0-0	
30		30	A	Ards	L	1-5	Curran 45' (pen)

Final League Position: 10th in the Irish Premier League

Appearances

Sub. Appearances

Goals

G. Cullen	S. Johnston	G. Fulton	S. Ferguson	P. McLaughlin	R. Boyle	A. Friel	D. Curran	P. Keenan	M. McHugh	B. Meehan	M. Ward	R. Casey	P. Donegan	C. McCullagh	T. Grant	C. Keenan	A. Coleman	C. Larkin	A. Young	P. Murphy	S. Murtagh	A. McDermott	R. Clarke	A. Crawford	M. McCann	R. Farrell	D. Donohoe	J. Quigley	R. McLaughlin	D. Cunningham	
1	2	3	4	5	6	7	8	9†	10*	11	12*	14†																			1
1	2	3	7*	5	6	12*	8	9		11	10	4																			2
1	2	3	7	5	6	14†	8	9†		11	10*	12*	4																		3
1	2	3		5	6†	7	8		9	11	10*	4*	12*	14†	15°																4
1	2	3	7	5			6	9*	10	12*		8	4	11																	5
1	2	3	14†	5			8	15°	10°	11	7†	4*	6	9		12*															6
1	2	3	15°	5		12*	8	14†	10°	11	7†	4	6	9*																	7
1	2	3	14†	5			8	12*	10	11	7†	4	6*	9																	8
	2*		7	5	3	15°	8	9	10°	11			14†	6		12*	1	4†													9
	2	4	7	5	3	12*	8	9†	10	11*		15°	14†	6°			1														10
	2	3	7	5	6	10†	8	15°	12*	11°			14†	9*			1														11
	2		7	5	6	14†	8	12*	10†	11*		4	3	9			1														12
	2		7	5	6	14†	8	12*	10†	11*		4	3	9			1														13
	2		7	5	6	12*	8		10	11*		4	3	9			1														14
	2		7	5	6	12*	8	14†	10*	11	15°	4	3	9		2†	1°														15
	2			5	6	7	8	4	10	11			3	9			1														16
	2		14†	5	15°	12*				11							1		3°			4	6	7	8†	9	10*				17
	2		7	5		12*	8		10†	11							1					3	6			9	4*	14†			18
			8	5	2	10°	3			11						15°	1					4	6	7*	14†	9†	12*				19
			8	5	2	10*	3			11							1		14†			4	6	7°	12*	9†	15°				20
			10	5	2		3		15°	11							1		14†			4†	6	7	8*	9°	12*				21
				5	3†		8	15°		11						10	1				2	4*	6	7		9°	12*	14†			22
			8	5	2	10*	11			12*						3	1					4	6	7		9†	14†				23
			8	5	2	7	3		12*	11							1					4	6			9	10*				24
			8	5	2*	7	3		15°	11						14†	1					4†	6	12*		9	10*				25
			8	5		14†	2		12*	11						10°	1		3			4	6	7*		9†			15°		26
			8	5	2	10	3			11						14†	1	1				4	6	7†		9*	12*				27
			8	5	2	10	3			11*						4	1						6	7†	12*	9	14†				28
			7	5	2	10	3		12*	11						4	1						6	14†		9†	8*				29
			8	5	2	7	3		10†	11*						4	1						6	14†		9°	15°			12*	30
8	17	10	23	30	23	13	29	7	15	26	6	11	11	13		6	14	1	7	1	4	11	14	10	3	13	4				Apps
	4		1	12		7	8	1	4	3	2	1	1	5							2			3	3		9	1	1	1	Subs
	1			1		2	4		3	8		2		4										1	2	4	5				Goals

77

Omagh Town FC
2004-2005 Season Statistics

#	Month	Date	H/A	Opponent	Result	Score	Scorers
1	Sep	25	A	Larne	L	0-2	
2	Oct	2	h	Loughgall	L	0-2	
3		9	H	Cliftonville	L	1-2	Johnston 65'
4		15	H	Newry City	D	2-2	Scanlon 68', Shields 90' (pen)
5		23	A	Portadown	L	0-9	
6		30	H	Limavady United	L	2-5	Donaghy 3', Shields 24' (pen)
7	Nov	6	A	Lisburn Distillery	L	1-6	Whitehead 63'
8		15	H	Linfield	L	1-8	Whitehead 84'
9		20	A	Ards	L	0-2	
10		27	H	Crusaders	L	1-3	Johnston 39'
11	Dec	4	A	Ballymena United	D	1-1	Whitehead 53'
12		11	H	Glentoran	L	2-3	Whitehead 60', Shields 86' (pen)
13		17	A	Institute	W	1-0	Clarke 19'
14		27	H	Dungannon Swifts	L	1-4	Johnston 79'
15	Jan	1	A	Coleraine	W	4-3	Canning 29', Cooke 32' 36', Lloyd 79'
16		3	H	Larne	W	3-0	Johnston 55' 78', Lloyd 83'
17		22	H	Cliftonville	L	0-5	
18		28	A	Newry City	L	1-2	Johnston 85'
19	Feb	1	A	Loughgall	W	3-1	Johnston 8', Ward 64', Cooke 90'
20		5	H	Portadown	L	1-2	Cooke 67'
21		19	A	Limavady United	L	0-2	
22		26	H	Lisburn Distillery	L	2-3	Shields 49' (pen), R. Mullan 82'
23	Mar	12	A	Linfield	L	1-6	Ward 32'
24		19	H	Ards	W	2-1	Hamilton 12', Ward 15'
25		24	A	Crusaders	L	1-3	Canning 37'
26		29	H	Ballymena United	L	0-2	
27	Apr	9	A	Glentoran	L	0-3	
28		16	H	Coleraine	L	1-3	Gaston 55' (og)
29		23	A	Dungannon Swifts	L	1-2	R. Mullan 33'
30		30	H	Institute	L	0-1	

Final League Position: 16th in the Irish Premier League

Appearances

Sub. Appearances

Goals

J. Connolly	G. Moore	E. Gilloway	T. Scanlon	S. Fanthorpe	R. Clarke	T. Shields	D. McCreadie	N. Johnston	N. Cooke	N. Bonner	D. Whitehead	R. McGinley	G. McCrory	S. Sweeney	A. McCarron	E. Kavanagh	J. Donaghy	D. Bradley	L. Farren	N. Lloyd	B. McElholm	G. Watson	C. Mullan	W. Patterson	A. Creane	B. Canning	L. Hamilton	G. Gill	M. Ward	R. Mullan	G. Woods	C. Green	M. Ferry	A. Morrow	
1	2	3	4	5	6	7	8	9°	10*	11†	12*	14†	15°																						1
1	2	3	4	5	6	7	8	9	10	11*	12*																								2
1	2*	3	4	5	6	7	8	9	10†	14†	11	12*																							3
1		2	4	5	6	7	8	9			10			3*	11	12*																			4
1		12*	4	5	6	7	2		10*	11	9				8	3																			5
1		3	2†	5	12*	6	7		11*	9	8				14†	10	4																		6
		2	4	5	6		11	10		8	9			3						7	1														7
		15°		5	6	7		10	14†	11†	12*			3*			4					1	2			8°									8
		2				6	7†	12*	10*	11	9	14†		3			4					1			5	8									9
		2				6	7	12*	10	11†	9			3			4					1			5	8*	14†								10
		2				6	7	8	12*	10	11*	9°		3†	15°		4					1			5	14†									11
		2				6*	7	8	10†	11	9			3°	14†	15°	4					1	12*		5										12
		2				6	7	8†	14†	10*	11	9		3			4					1	12*		5										13
						7	8	10	12*	11	9			3			4	5*	6			1	2												14
						6		12*	9*	10	15°	14†		11			4°			7		1	2	3	5	8†									15
						6		12*	9	10†		14†		11*			4			7		1	2	3	4	8									16
		2				6*		12*	9	11†			15°				4°			7		1		3	5	8			10	14†					17
						6			9					11†			4			7*		1	2	3	5	8			10	12*	14†				18
						6			9		12*						4			7		1	2	3*	5	8†			10	14†		11			19
						6			9	14†	15°								12*	7†		1	2*	3	5	8			10			11°	4		20
						6°			9								4			7		1		3†	5	12*	8*		10	14†		15°	11	2	21
						6			9								14†		3°	7		1	15°		5	8*	12*		4	11†		2			22
						6		12*	11		15°						4			7		1	5°	8	9*	14†			10	3†		2			23
		2				6†		12*	11											7°		1	5	3	8	9*	14†		10	4		15°			24
		2†				6		12*	11		15°									7*		1	5	3°	9	8			10	14†		4			25
		2†				6		12*	9°	11*							4			7		1	5		8	15°	14†		10	3					26
									9	8*	11†	6°					4			7°		1	2	3		12*	14†		10	5		15°			27
						6			9*		12*						4			7°		1	15°	3	8	14†			10	5		11†	2		28
						6			9	15°	11*						8					1	2	3	14†	7°			10°	5		12*	4		29
						6	14†		9°	11							5			7		1	2	3		12*	8*		10†			15°	4		30
6	3	15	8	7	12	26	14	17	15	19	10	12	8	4	2	3	11	4	7	19	1	20	12	13	9	12	4	4	13	4	1	6	9		
	1	1		1		3	8	7	3	3	6	5	3	1	1				2	2		1	1			7	4	1	2	3	3	1	1		
		1		1	4			7	4		4					1				2					2	1			3	2					

Portadown FC
2004-2005 Season Statistics

1	Sep	25	A	Glentoran	W	2-1	Hamilton 4', Arkins 13'
2	Oct	2	H	Larne	W	3-0	Arkins 51', Neill 54', P. McCann 67'
3		9	A	Institute	L	1-2	Clarke 87'
4		16	H	Cliftonville	W	3-0	Hamilton 50', P. McCann 55', Arkins 72'
5		23	H	Omagh Town	W	9-0	Hamilton 2' 21' 49' 56' 62' 68', Kelly 45', P. McCann 46' 90'
6		30	A	Lisburn Distillery	L	0-2	
7	Nov	6	H	Ballymena United	W	3-0	P. McCann 5', Convery 71', Hamilton 81'
8		13	H	Limavady United	L	0-1	
9		20	A	Crusaders	W	1-0	Hamilton 85'
10		27	A	Ards	W	1-0	Neill 10'
11	Dec	4	H	Linfield	L	0-1	
12		11	H	Coleraine	W	2-0	Boyle 4' 45'
13		18	A	Dungannon Swifts	W	3-1	Heffernan 54' (og), Craig 63', M. McCann 90'
14		27	H	Loughgall	D	2-2	Kelly 43', P. McCann 70'
15		30	A	Newry City	W	6-0	M. McCann 11' 46' 82', Neill 19', Arkins 70', Boyle 84'
16	Jan	3	H	Glentoran	W	4-3	Arkins 34', M. McCann 43' 72', O'Hara 88'
17		8	A	Larne	W	3-2	Convery 8', Boyle 78', Arkins 82'
18		22	H	Institute	W	4-0	Arkins 15' 54', M. McCann 48', Clarke 62'
19		29	A	Cliftonville	W	2-0	Arkins 26' 40'
20	Feb	5	A	Omagh Town	W	2-1	Arkins 52' 76'
21		19	H	Lisburn Distillery	W	2-1	Quinn 77', Arkins 88'
22		26	A	Ballymena United	L	0-2	
23	Mar	12	A	Limavady United	W	2-0	Arkins 27', M. McCann 47'
24		19	H	Crusaders	D	0-0	
25		25	H	Ards	L	2-3	Arkins 13' (pen), Lindsay 33'
26		29	A	Linfield	D	0-0	
27	Apr	8	A	Coleraine	D	2-2	Hamilton 64', P. McCann 68'
28		16	H	Newry City	L	2-3	M. McCann 37', Hamilton 54'
29		21	A	Loughgall	W	2-0	McCordick 19', Quinn 30'
30		30	H	Dungannon Swifts	L	1-2	Feeney 26'

Final League Position: 3rd in the Irish Premier League

Appearances

Sub. Appearances

Goals

D. Miskelly	P. Craig	K. O'Hara	R. Clarke	J. Convery	D. Kelly	P. McCann	M. Collins	G. Hamilton	V. Arkins	K. Neill	M. McCann	K. Lindsay	W. Boyle	C. Feeney	N. Alerdice	S. McCordick	R. Harpur	P. Quinn	P. Murphy	C. McAnallen	A. Teggart	
1	2	3	4°	5†	6	7	8	9	10	11*	12*	14†	15°									1
1	2	3	4	5	6	7	8	9*	10	11		12*										2
1	2†	3	4	5	6	7	8		10	11	12*	14†	9*									3
1		3	4*	5	6	7	8†	9°	10	12*	11	14†	15°	2								4
1		3	4*	5	6	7	8°	9	10	15°	11	14†	12*		2†							5
1		3	4	5	6	7	8*	9	10†	11		14†	12*	2								6
1		3	4†	10	6		8	9		11*	12*	5	14†	2								7
1		3	4	10	6	7	8†	9		11*	12*	5	14†	2°	15°							8
1	2	3	4	5	6	7†	8	9		11	12*	14†	10*									9
1	2	3	4	10	6	7	8	9		11		5										10
1	2	3		10	6	7°	8	9		11†	12*	5	4*		15°	14†						11
1		3	4	5	6	7*	8	12*		11	9		10	2								12
1	12*	3†	4	5	6	7	8			11	9	14†	10	2*								13
1	2	3	4	9*	6	7	8		12*	11		5	10									14
1	2	3°	4*	5	6		8		10	11†	9		7		14†	12*	15°					15
1	2†	3	4	5	6	12*	8		10	11*	9		7		14†							16
1		3	4†	5	6	12*	8		10	11*	9		7	2				14†				17
1		3°	4	5	6†	7*	8		10	11	9	14†		2	15°			12*				18
1		3	4	5	6	7		12*	10	11	9†	14†		2				8*				19
1		3	4	5	6°	7†	8	12*	10	11*	9	15°		2				14†				20
1		3	4	5	6	7	8	12*	10	11†	9			2*				14†				21
1		3	4	5	6	12*	8°	9	10	15°	11		7*	2†				14†				22
		3			6	7	8		10	11	9	5		2				4	1			23
		3		5	6	7	8*	14†	10	11†	9°	15°	12*	2				4	1			24
	2	3	4	5		7*		9†	10	11	14†	6	8					12*	1			25
		4	5*	6†		7		9		3	11	14†	8	2		12*		10	1			26
	5					7		9		3†	10*	4	12*	14†	8			6	1	2	11	27
	5					7	12*	9	10		6	4	14†	2°		15°		8†	1	3	11*	28
1	5	15°				7	8*	9†			6	14†				2°	10	12*	4	3	11	29
	5	6†				7		9			10*	4	11°	2		12*	14†	8	1	3	15°	30
23	14	25	24	25	25	26	24	17	18	22	20	11	13	16	4	1		8	7	4	3	Apps
	1		1			3	1	5	1	3	7	12	11	3	4	4	3	6			1	Subs
	1	1	2	2	2	7		12	15	3	9	1	4	1		1		2				Goals

Irish Premier League Fixtures 2005/2006

Saturday 17th September 2005

Ards vs Cliftonville
Armagh City vs Institute
Ballymena United vs Larne
Dungannon Swifts vs Loughgall
Limavady United vs Coleraine
Linfield vs Glenavon
Lisburn Distillery vs Glentoran
Portadown vs Newry City

Saturday 24th September 2005

Cliftonville vs Portadown
Coleraine vs Lisburn Distillery
Glenavon vs Dungannon Swifts
Glentoran vs Ards
Institute vs Linfield
Larne vs Armagh City
Loughgall vs Limavady United
Newry City vs Ballymena United

Saturday 1st October 2005

Ards vs Institute
Armagh City vs Newry City
Ballymena United vs Cliftonville
Dungannon Swifts vs Larne
Limavady United vs Glentoran
Linfield vs Coleraine
Lisburn Distillery vs Glenavon
Portadown vs Loughgall

Saturday 15th October 2005

Cliftonville vs Linfield
Coleraine vs Portadown
Glenavon vs Ards
Glentoran vs Armagh City
Institute vs Dungannon Swifts
Larne vs Limavady United
Loughgall vs Ballymena United
Newry City vs Lisburn Distillery

Saturday 22nd October 2005

Armagh City vs Ballymena United
Cliftonville vs Newry City
Coleraine vs Glentoran
Glenavon vs Loughgall
Institute vs Larne
Limavady United vs Dungannon Swifts
Linfield vs Ards
Lisburn Distillery vs Portadown

Saturday 29th October 2005

Ards vs Armagh City
Ballymena United vs Linfield
Dungannon Swifts vs Lisburn Distillery
Glentoran vs Cliftonville
Larne vs Coleraine
Loughgall vs Institute
Newry City vs Glenavon
Portadown vs Limavady United

Saturday 5th November 2005

Ballymena United vs Dungannon Swifts
Cliftonville vs Loughgall
Coleraine vs Glenavon
Institute vs Glentoran
Larne vs Newry City
Linfield vs Limavady United
Lisburn Distillery vs Armagh City
Portadown vs Ards

Saturday 12th November 2005

Ards vs Ballymena United
Armagh City vs Portadown
Dungannon Swifts vs Linfield
Glenavon vs Cliftonville
Glentoran vs Larne
Limavady United vs Lisburn Distillery
Loughgall vs Coleraine
Newry City vs Institute

Saturday 19th November 2005

Ballymena United vs Limavady United
Coleraine vs Cliftonville
Institute vs Glenavon
Larne vs Loughgall
Linfield vs Armagh City
Lisburn Distillery vs Ards
Newry City vs Glentoran
Portadown vs Dungannon Swifts

Saturday 26th November 2005

Ards vs Limavady United
Armagh City vs Dungannon Swifts
Ballymena United vs Lisburn Distillery
Cliftonville vs Larne
Coleraine vs Institute
Glenavon vs Glentoran
Linfield vs Portadown
Loughgall vs Newry City

Friday 2nd December 2005

Dungannon Swifts vs Ards
Glentoran vs Loughgall
Institute vs Cliftonville
Larne vs Glenavon
Limavady United vs Armagh City
Lisburn Distillery vs Linfield
Newry City vs Coleraine
Portadown vs Ballymena United

Saturday 10th December 2005

Cliftonville vs Limavady United
Coleraine vs Dungannon Swifts
Glenavon vs Armagh City
Glentoran vs Ballymena United
Institute vs Portadown
Larne vs Lisburn Distillery
Loughgall vs Linfield
Newry City vs Ards

Saturday 17th December 2005

Ards vs Loughgall
Armagh City vs Coleraine
Ballymena United vs Glenavon
Dungannon Swifts vs Cliftonville
Limavady United vs Newry City
Linfield vs Larne
Lisburn Distillery vs Institute
Portadown vs Glentoran

Monday, 26th December 2005

Cliftonville vs Lisburn Distillery
Coleraine vs Ballymena United
Glenavon vs Portadown
Glentoran vs Linfield
Institute vs Limavady United
Larne vs Ards
Loughgall vs Armagh City
Newry City vs Dungannon Swifts

Saturday 31st December 2005

Ards vs Coleraine
Armagh City vs Cliftonville
Ballymena United vs Institute
Dungannon Swifts vs Glentoran
Limavady United vs Glenavon
Linfield vs Newry City
Lisburn Distillery vs Loughgall
Portadown vs Larne

Monday 2nd January 2006

Cliftonville vs Ards
Coleraine vs Limavady United
Glenavon vs Linfield
Glentoran vs Lisburn Distillery
Institute vs Armagh City
Larne vs Ballymena United
Loughgall vs Dungannon Swifts
Newry City vs Portadown

Saturday 7th January 2006

Ards vs Glentoran
Armagh City vs Larne
Ballymena United vs Newry City
Dungannon Swifts vs Glenavon
Limavady United vs Loughgall
Linfield vs Institute
Lisburn Distillery vs Coleraine
Portadown vs Cliftonville

Saturday 21st January 2006

Cliftonville vs Ballymena United
Coleraine vs Linfield
Glenavon vs Lisburn Distillery
Glentoran vs Limavady United
Institute vs Ards
Larne vs Dungannon Swifts
Loughgall vs Portadown
Newry City vs Armagh City

Saturday 28th January 2006

Ards vs Glenavon
Armagh City vs Glentoran
Ballymena United vs Loughgall
Dungannon Swifts vs Institute
Limavady United vs Larne
Linfield vs Cliftonville
Lisburn Distillery vs Newry City
Portadown vs Coleraine

Saturday 4th February 2006

Ards vs Linfield
Ballymena United vs Armagh City
Dungannon Swifts vs Limavady United
Glentoran vs Coleraine
Larne vs Institute
Loughgall vs Glenavon
Newry City vs Cliftonville
Portadown vs Lisburn Distillery

Saturday 18th February 2006

Armagh City vs Ards
Cliftonville vs Glentoran
Coleraine vs Larne
Glenavon vs Newry City
Institute vs Loughgall
Limavady United vs Portadown
Linfield vs Ballymena United
Lisburn Distillery vs Dungannon Swifts

Saturday 25th February 2006

Ards vs Portadown
Armagh City vs Lisburn Distillery
Dungannon Swifts vs Ballymena United
Glenavon vs Coleraine
Glentoran vs Institute
Limavady United vs Linfield
Loughgall vs Cliftonville
Newry City vs Larne

Saturday 11th March 2006

Ballymena United vs Ards
Cliftonville vs Glenavon
Coleraine vs Loughgall
Institute vs Newry City
Larne vs Glentoran
Linfield vs Dungannon Swifts
Lisburn Distillery vs Limavady United
Portadown vs Armagh City

Saturday 18th March 2006

Ards vs Lisburn Distillery
Armagh City vs Linfield
Cliftonville vs Coleraine
Dungannon Swifts vs Portadown
Glenavon vs Institute
Glentoran vs Newry City
Limavady United vs Ballymena United
Loughgall vs Larne

Saturday 25th March 2006

Dungannon Swifts vs Armagh City
Glentoran vs Glenavon
Institute vs Coleraine
Larne vs Cliftonville
Limavady United vs Ards
Lisburn Distillery vs Ballymena United
Newry City vs Loughgall
Portadown vs Linfield

Saturday 8th April 2006	Ards vs Dungannon Swifts
	Armagh City vs Limavady United
	Ballymena United vs Portadown
	Cliftonville vs Institute
	Coleraine vs Newry City
	Glenavon vs Larne
	Linfield vs Lisburn Distillery
	Loughgall vs Glentoran
Saturday 15th April 2006	Ards vs Larne
	Armagh City vs Loughgall
	Ballymena United vs Coleraine
	Dungannon Swifts vs Newry City
	Limavady United vs Institute
	Linfield vs Glentoran
	Lisburn Distillery vs Cliftonville
	Portadown vs Glenavon
Tuesday, 18th April 2006	Cliftonville vs Dungannon Swifts
	Coleraine vs Armagh City
	Glenavon vs Ballymena United
	Glentoran vs Portadown
	Institute vs Lisburn Distillery
	Larne vs Linfield
	Loughgall vs Ards
	Newry City vs Limavady United
Saturday 22nd April 2006	Ards vs Newry City
	Armagh City vs Glenavon
	Ballymena United vs Glentoran
	Dungannon Swifts vs Coleraine
	Limavady United vs Cliftonville
	Linfield vs Loughgall
	Lisburn Distillery vs Larne
	Portadown vs Institute
Saturday 29th April 2006	Cliftonville vs Armagh City
	Coleraine vs Ards
	Glenavon vs Limavady United
	Glentoran vs Dungannon Swifts
	Institute vs Ballymena United
	Larne vs Portadown
	Loughgall vs Lisburn Distillery
	Newry City vs Linfield

18th February 2004
v NORWAY (FR) *Windsor Park*

M. Taylor	Birmingham City
C. Baird	Southampton
P. Kennedy	Wigan Athletic (sub. S. Jones)
A. Hughes	Newcastle United
G. McCartney	Sunderland
D. Griffin	Stockport County (sub. M. Williams)
K. Gillespie	Leicester City (sub. P. McVeigh)
D. Johnson	Birmingham City
D. Healy	Preston North End
A. Smith	Glentoran
M. Hughes	Crystal Palace

Result 1-4   Healy

31st March 2004
v ESTONIA (FR) *Tallinn*

M. Taylor	Birmingham City
C. Baird	Southampton
T. Capaldi	Plymouth Argyle
S. Craigan	Motherwell
M. Williams	Wimbledon
D. Sonner	Nottingham Forest (sub. M. Duff)
P. Mulryne	Norwich City (sub. G. McCann)
J. Whitley	Sunderland
D. Healy	Preston North End
A. Smith	Glentoran
S. Jones	Crewe Alexandra

Result 1-0   Healy

28th April 2004
v SERBIA & MONTENEGRO (FR)
Windsor Park

M. Taylor	Birmingham City (sub. R. Carroll)
C. Baird	Southampton
T. Capaldi	Plymouth Argyle
S. Craigan	Motherwell
M. Williams	Wimbledon
T. Doherty	Bristol City (sub. M. Hughes)
K. Gillespie	Leicester City (sub. S. Jones)
J. Whitley	Sunderland (sub. D. Sonner)
D. Healy	Preston North End (sub. G. Hamilton)
J. Quinn	Willem II (sub. A. Smith)
P. Mulryne	Norwich City (sub. P. McVeigh)

Result 1-1   Quinn

30th May 2004
v BARBADOS (FR) *Waterford*

M. Taylor	Birmingham City
C. Baird	Southampton (sub. S. Jones)
T. Capaldi	Plymouth Argyle (sub. S. Elliott)
S. Craigan	Motherwell
M. Williams	Wimbledon
D. Johnson	Birmingham City
K. Gillespie	Leicester City (sub. C. Murdock)
D. Sonner	Nottingham Forest (sub. P. McVeigh)
D. Healy	Preston North End (sub. G. Hamilton)
J. Quinn	Willem II
P. Mulryne	Norwich City (sub. A. Smith)

Result 1-1 Healy

2nd June 2004
v ST. KITTS & NEVIS (FR)
Basseterre

M. Taylor	Birmingham City
C. Baird	Southampton
T. Capaldi	Plymouth Argyle
S. Craigan	Motherwell
C. Murdock	Hibernian
J. Whitley	Sunderland (sub. D. Johnson)
P. McVeigh	Norwich City (sub. P. Mulryne)
D. Sonner	Nottingham Forest (sub. S. Jones)
G. Hamilton	Portadown (sub. D. Healy)
A. Smith	Glentoran
S. Elliott	Hull City (sub. K. Gillespie)

Result 3-0   Healy, Jones

6th June 2004
v TRINIDAD & TOBAGO (FR)
Bacolet

M. Taylor	Birmingham City (sub. A. Mannus)
C. Baird	Southampton
T. Capaldi	Plymouth Argyle
S. Craigan	Motherwell (sub. C. Murdock)
M. Williams	Wimbledon
J. Whitley	Sunderland
D. Johnson	Birmingham City (sub. K. Gillespie)
P. Mulryne	Norwich City (sub. D. Sonner)
D. Healy	Preston North End (sub. P. McVeigh)
J. Quinn	Willem II (sub. A. Smith)
S. Elliott	Hull City (sub. S. Jones)

Result 3-0   Healy 2, Elliott

NORTHERN IRELAND INTERNATIONAL LINE-UPS AND STATISTICS 2004-2005

18th August 2004
v SWITZERLAND (FR) *Zurich*

R. Carroll	Manchester United
A. Hughes	Newcastle United
T. Capaldi	Plymouth Argyle
S. Craigan	Motherwell (sub M. Duff)
M. Williams	MK Dons (sub C. Murdock)
D. Johnson	Birmingham City
K. Gillespie	Leicester City (sub P. McVeigh)
D. Sonnor	Peterborough United
D. Healy	Preston North End (sub G. Hamilton)
A. Smith	Preston North End
S. Elliott	Hull City (sub C. Brunt)

Result 0-0

4th September 2004
v POLAND (WCQ) *Windsor Park*

M. Taylor	Birmingham City
A. Hughes	Newcastle United
T. Capaldi	Plymouth Argyle
S. Craigan	Motherwell
M. Williams	MK Dons
D. Johnson	Birmingham City
S. Elliott	Hull City (sub P. McVeigh)
J. Whitley	Sunderland
D. Healy	Preston North End
J. Quinn	Willem II (sub A. Smith)
M. Hughes	Crystal Palace (sub S. Jones)

Result 0-3

8th September 2004
v WALES (WCQ) *Millennium Stadium*

M. Taylor	Birmingham City
M. Clyde	Wolves
T. Capaldi	Plymouth Argyle (sub G. McCartney)
C. Murdock	Hibernian
M. Williams	MK Dons
A. Hughes	Newcastle United
D. Johnson	Birmingham City
J. Whitley	Sunderland
D. Healy	Preston North End
J. Quinn	Willem II (sub A. Smith (sub P. McVeigh)
M. Hughes	Crystal Palace

Result 2-2   Whitley, Healy

9th October 2004
v AZERBAIJAN (WCQ) *Baku*

M. Taylor	Birmingham City
C. Baird	Southampton (sub K. Gillespie)
M. Clyde	Wolves
M. Williams	MK Dons
C. Murdock	Hibernian
A. Hughes	Newcastle United
D. Johnson	Birmingham City
T. Doherty	Bristol City
J. Whitley	Sunderland
J. Quinn	Willem II (sub A. Smith)
S. Elliott	Hull City

Result 0-0

13th October 2004
v AUSTRIA (WCQ) *Windsor Park*

R. Carroll	Manchester United
A. Hughes	Newcastle United
G. McCartney	Sunderland
M. Williams	MK Dons
C. Murdock	Hibernian (sub S. Elliott)
D. Johnson	Birmingham City
K. Gillespie	Leicester City
T. Doherty	Bristol City (sub S. Jones)
D. Healy	Preston North End
J. Quinn	Willem II
J. Whitley	Sunderland (sub P. McVeigh)

Result 3-3   Healy, Murdock, Elliott

9th February 2005
v CANADA (FR) *Windsor Park*

M. Taylor	Birmingham City (sub R. Carroll)
C. Baird	Southampton
T. Capaldi	Plymouth Argyle (sub S. Craigan)
G. McCartney	Sunderland
A. Hughes	Newcastle United
C. Murdock	Crewe Alexandra (sub A. Kirk)
T. Doherty	Bristol City (sub P. Mulryne)
K. Gillespie	Leicester City (sub S. Jones)
J. Whitley	Sunderland
D. Healy	Leeds United (sub A. Smith)
S. Davis	Aston Villa

Result 0-1

26th March 2005

v ENGLAND (WCQ) *Old Trafford*

M. Taylor	Birmingham City
C. Baird	Southampton
T. Capaldi	Plymouth Argyle
A. Hughes	Newcastle United
C. Murdock	Crewe Alexandra
D. Johnson	Birmingham City
K. Gillespie	Leicester City
J. Whitley	Sunderland (sub S. Jones)
D. Healy	Leeds United (sub A. Kirk)
T. Doherty	Bristol City (sub S. Davis)
S. Elliott	Hull City

Result 0-4

30th March 2005

v POLAND (WCQ) *Warsaw*

M. Taylor	Birmingham City
C. Baird	Southampton
T. Capaldi	Plymouth Argyle
M. Williams	MK Dons (sub S. Elliott)
C. Murdock	Crewe Alexandra
A. Hughes	Newcastle United
K. Gillespie	Leicester City
S. Davis	Aston Villa
D. Healy	Leeds United (sub A. Smith)
J. Quinn	Sheffield Wednesday (sub W. Feeney)
J. Whitley	Sunderland

Result 0-1

4th June 2005

v GERMANY (FR) *Windsor Park*

M. Taylor	Birmingham City (sub M. Ingham)
C. Baird	Southampton
M. Clyde	Wolves
S. Craigan	Motherwell (sub C. Brunt)
G. McCartney	Sunderland
D. Johnson	Birmingham City
K. Gillespie	Leicester City (sub G. McAuley)
S. Davis	Aston Villa
D. Healy	Leeds United (sub A. Smith)
S. Jones	Crewe Alexandra (sub A. Kirk)
S. Elliott	Hull City (sub W. Feeney)

Result 1-4 Healy (pen)

Irish Cup 2004/2005

Prelim. Round	18th Sep 2004	Abbey Villa	3	Albert Foundry	5
Prelim. Round	18th Sep 2004	Annagh United	3	Laurelvale	0
Prelim. Round	18th Sep 2004	Ballynahinch United	2	Roe Valley	1
Prelim. Round	18th Sep 2004	Barn United	1	Blackers Mill	3
Prelim. Round	18th Sep 2004	Bryansburn Rangers	3	Rasharkin United	'6
Prelim. Round	18th Sep 2004	CKU	3	Dunmurry Young Men	0
Prelim. Round	18th Sep 2004	Dergview	7	Broomhedge	0
Prelim. Round	18th Sep 2004	Downpatrick FC	6	Dromore Amateurs	2
Prelim. Round	18th Sep 2004	Downshire Youmg Men	3	Sirocco Works	4
Prelim. Round	18th Sep 2004	Fivemiletown United	3	Bangor Amateurs ??	
Prelim. Round	18th Sep 2004	Glebe Rangers	0	Lisburn Rangers	2
Prelim. Round	18th Sep 2004	Grove United	1	Dundonald	0
Prelim. Round	18th Sep 2004	Islandmagee	4	Markethill Swifts	1
Prelim. Round	18th Sep 2004	Killymoon Rangers	1	Donard Hospital	2
Prelim. Round	18th Sep 2004	Larne Tech Old Boys	3	Newbuildings	2
Prelim. Round	18th Sep 2004	Malachians	11	Banbridge AFC	0
Prelim. Round	18th Sep 2004	Newington Youth Club	2	Holywood FC	3
Prelim. Round	18th Sep 2004	Orangefield Old Boys	0	Nortel	3
Prelim. Round	18th Sep 2004	Oxford United Stars	4	Draperstown Celtic	3
Prelim. Round	18th Sep 2004	Portadown BBOB	0	Ballymacash Rangers	1
Prelim. Round	18th Sep 2004	Rosario	3	Civil Service	1
Prelim. Round	18th Sep 2004	Seagoe United	0	Magherafelt Sky Blues	1
Prelim. Round	18th Sep 2004	Shorts	2	Warrenpoint Town	4
Prelim. Round	18th Sep 2004	Sperrin Olympic	3	Ballycastle United	0
Prelim. Round	18th Sep 2004	Strabane	2	Hanover	0
Prelim. Round	18th Sep 2004	Wellington Rec.	4	Tandragee Rovers	1
Prelim. Round	18th Sep 2004	UUC	0	Desertmartin	4
Round 1	9th Oct 2004	Albert Foundry	4	Rosario Youth Club	1
Round 1	9th Oct 2004	Annagh United	1	Lisburn Rangers	3
Round 1	9th Oct 2004	Dergview	4	Grove United	0
Round 1	9th Oct 2004	Desertmartin	1	Sirocco Works	2
Round 1	9th Oct 2004	Donard Hospital	1	CKU	2
Round 1	9th Oct 2004	Downpatrick	5	Blackers Mill	0
Round 1	9th Oct 2004	Holywood	1	Malachians	4
Round 1	9th Oct 2004	Larne Tech Old Boys	5	Fivemiletown United	0
Round 1	9th Oct 2004	Magherafelt Sky Blues	3	Wellington Rec.	0
Round 1	9th Oct 2004	Nortel	3	Islandmagee	0
Round 1	9th Oct 2004	Rasharkin United	4	Oxford United Stars	3
Round 1	9th Oct 2004	Saintfield United	0	Ballymacash Rangers	2
Round 1	9th Oct 2004	Strabane	2	Sperrin Olympic	1
Round 1	9th Oct 2004	Warrenpoint Town	1	Ballynahinch United	2
Round 2	30th Oct 2004	Albert Foundry	2	Rasharkin United	1
Round 2	30th Oct 2004	Ballymacash Rangers	1	Ballynahinch United	4
Round 2	30th Oct 2004	Dergview	2	Larne Tech OB	3
Round 2	30th Oct 2004	Downpatrick	1	Strabane	2
Round 2	30th Oct 2004	Magherafelt Sky Blues	2	CKU	0
Round 2	30th Oct 2004	Malachians	1	Lisburn Rangers	1
		(Lisburn Rangers won 5-4 on penalties)			
Round 2	30th Oct 2004	Nortel	2	Sirocco Works	3

Round 3	13th Nov 2004	1st Bangor Old Boys	2	Dromara Village	4
Round 3	13th Nov 2004	Ards Rangers	0	Kilmore Recreation	1
Round 3	13th Nov 2004	Ballymoney United	1	Portstewart	0
Round 3	13th Nov 2004	Ballynahinch United	2	Strabane	1
Round 3	13th Nov 2004	Banbridge Town	4	Queens University	1
Round 3	13th Nov 2004	Chimney Corner	0	East Belfast	2
Round 3	13th Nov 2004	Coagh United	1	Albert Foundry	0
Round 3	13th Nov 2004	Comber Recreation	2	Crewe United	1
Round 3	13th Nov 2004	Crumlin United	1	Ballinamallard United	2
Round 3	13th Nov 2004	Dundela	2	Brantwood	0
Round 3	13th Nov 2004	Dunmurry Recreation	2	Donegal Celtic	2
Round 3	13th Nov 2004	FC Enkalon	1	Knockbreda Parish	2
Round 3	13th Nov 2004	Harland & Wolff Welders	2	Drumaness Mills	1
Round 3	13th Nov 2004	Larne Tech Old Boys	2	Rathfriland Rangers	0
Round 3	13th Nov 2004	Lisburn Rangers	2	Killyleagh Youth Club	0
Round 3	13th Nov 2004	Magherafelt Sky Blues	0	Moyola Park	1
Round 3	13th Nov 2004	PSNI	1	Sirocco Works	2
Round 3	13th Nov 2004	Wakehurst	3	Lurgan Celtic	1
Round 4	4th Dec 2004	Banbridge Town	2	Ballynahinch United	1
Round 4	4th Dec 2004	Coagh United	3	Sirocco Works	0
Round 4	4th Dec 2004	Donegal Celtic	2	Wakehurst	0
Round 4	4th Dec 2004	Dundela	1	Ballinamallard United	3
Round 4	4th Dec 2004	Harland & Wolff Welders	3	Dromara Village	0
Round 4	4th Dec 2004	Knockbreda Parish	2	East Belfast	3
Round 4	4th Dec 2004	Larne Tech Old Boys	2	Ballymoney United	4
Round 4	4th Dec 2004	Lisburn Rangers	3	Comber Recreation	0
Round 4	4th Dec 2004	Mouola Park	0	Kilmore Recreation	1
Round 5	15th Jan 2005	Armagh City	1	Dungannon Swifts	2
Round 5	15th Jan 2005	Ballyclare Comrades	1	Ards	1
Round 5	15th Jan 2005	Ballymena United	1	Coagh United	0
Round 5	15th Jan 2005	Bangor	1	Newry City	5
		Newry City were dismissed from the competition for fielding an ineligible player.			
Round 5	15th Jan 2005	Carrick Rangers	1	Coleraine	5
Round 5	15th Jan 2005	Cliftonville	2	Banbridge Town	3
Round 5	15th Jan 2005	Glenavon	0	Portadown	2
Round 5	15th Jan 2005	Glentoran	6	Lisburn Rangers	0
Round 5	15th Jan 2005	Institute	4	Ballymoney United	0
Round 5	15th Jan 2005	Kilmore Recreation	1	Ballynure Old Boys	0
Round 5	15th Jan 2005	Larne	3	East Belfast	0
Round 5	15th Jan 2005	Linfield	1	Limavady United	1
Round 5	15th Jan 2005	Lisburn Distillery	4	Ballinamallard United	1
Round 5	15th Jan 2005	Loughgall	5	Donegal Celtic	1
Round 5	15th Jan 2005	Omagh Town	0	Crusaders	1
Round 5	15th Jan 2005	Tobermore United	0	Harland & Wolff Welders	2
Replay	18th Jan 2005	Limavady United	1	Linfield	2
Replay	19th Jan 2005	Ballyclare Comrades	0	Ards	1
Round 6	12th Feb 2005	Ballymena United	4	Kilmore Recreation	1
Round 6	12th Feb 2005	Crusaders	0	Coleraine	1
Round 6	12th Feb 2005	Dungannon Swifts	1	Larne	2
Round 6	12th Feb 2005	Glentoran	1	Linfield	1

Round 6	12th Feb 2005	Institute	1	Ards	2
Round 6	12th Feb 2005	Lisburn Distillery	1	Harland & Wolff Welders	1
Round 6	12th Feb 2005	Loughgall	0	Banbridge Town	0
Round 6	1st Mar 2005	Portadown	2	Bangor	1
Replay	15th Feb 2005	Linfield	0	Glentoran	3
Replay	15th Feb 2005	Lisburn Distillery	1	Harland & Wolff Welders	2
Replay	15th Feb 2005	Loughgall	2	Banbridge Town	0
Quarter-Final	5th Mar 2005	Ards	0	Portadown	1
Quarter-Final	5th Mar 2005	Ballymena United	0	Harland & Wolff Welders	0
Quarter-Final	5th Mar 2005	Coleraine	1	Glentoran	2
Quarter-Final	5th Mar 2005	Loughgall	1	Larne	1
Replay	8th Mar 2005	Ballymena United	4	Harland & Wolff Welders	0
Replay	8th Mar 2005	Larne	3	Loughgall	0
Semi-Final	2nd Apr 2005	Ballymena United	0	Larne	1
Semi-Final	2nd Apr 2005	Glentoran	0	Portadown	0
Replay	5th Apr 2005	Portadown	1	Glentoran	0
FINAL	7th May 2005	Portadown	5	Larne	1
		Scorers: Atkins 15, 59, Convery 34, Kelly 36, M. McCann 48		Scorer: Ogden 3	

Portadown: Murphy, Feeney (Quinn 81), O'Hara, Clarke, Convery, Kelly, Boyle, Collins, M. McCann (Hamilton 46), Arkins, Neill (P. McCann 49).

Larne: Spackman, Small, Hughes, Curran, Murphy, Rodgers (Tumilty 72), Ogden, Weir (Parker 53), Hamlin, Dickson, Bonner (Crossley 53).

Referee: D. Malcolm (Bangor)

CIS Insurance Cup 2004

Section A	14th Aug 2004	Crusaders	3	Loughgall	0
Section A	14th Aug 2004	Linfield	0	Ards	0
Section A	21st Aug 2004	Ards	3	Crusaders	2
Section A	21st Aug 2004	Loughgall	1	Linfield	2
Section A	28th Aug 2004	Ards	0	Loughgall	0
Section A	28th Aug 2004	Crusaders	0	Linfield	2
Section A	11th Sep 2004	Linfield	4	Crusaders	0
Section A	11th Sep 2004	Loughgall	1	Ards	0
Section A	18th Sep 2004	Crusaders	2	Ards	0
Section A	18th Sep 2004	Linfield	5	Loughgall	1
Section A	21st Sep 2004	Ards	1	Linfield	2
Section A	21st Sep 2004	Loughgall	1	Crusaders	1

Section A – Final Table

	P	W	D	L	F	A	Pts	GD
1. Linfield (QF)	6	5	1	0	15	3	16	+12
2. Ards (QF)	6	2	1	3	6	7	7	-1
3. Crusaders	6	2	1	3	7	10	7	-3
4. Loughgall	6	1	1	4	4	12	4	-8

Section B	14th Aug 2004	Cliftonville	1	Limavady United	1
Section B	14th Aug 2004	Dungannon Swifts	2	Portadown	1
Section B	21st Aug 2004	Limavady United	1	Dungannon Swifts	2
Section B	21st Aug 2004	Portadown	0	Cliftonville	1
Section B	27th Aug 2004	Dungannon Swifts	0	Cliftonville	0
Section B	28th Aug 2004	Portadown	3	Limavady United	1
Section B	11th Sep 2004	Cliftonville	2	Dungannon Swifts	0
Section B	11th Sep 2004	Limavady United	1	Portadown	3
Section B	18th Sep 2004	Cliftonville	1	Portadown	3
Section B	18th Sep 2004	Dungannon Swifts	3	Limavady United	1
Section B	21st Sep 2004	Limavady United	1	Cliftonville	3
Section B	21st Sep 2004	Portadown	1	Dungannon Swifts	1

Section B – Final Table

	P	W	D	L	F	A	Pts	GD
1. Cliftonville (QF)	6	3	2	1	8	5	11	+3
2. Dungannon Swifts (QF)	6	3	2	1	8	6	11	+2
3. Portadown	6	3	1	2	11	7	10	+4
4. Limavady United	6	0	1	5	6	15	1	-9

Section C	13th Aug 2004	Larne	0	Institute	3
Section C	14th Aug 2004	Lisburn Distillery	2	Ballymena United	2
Section C	21st Aug 2004	Ballymena United	1	Larne	3
Section C	21st Aug 2004	Institute	0	Lisburn Distillery	2
Section C	28th Aug 2004	Ballymena United	3	Institute	0
Section C	28th Aug 2004	Larne	0	Lisburn Distillery	5
Section C	11th Sep 2004	Institute	1	Ballymena United	1
Section C	11th Sep 2004	Lisburn Distillery	0	Larne	1
Section C	18th Sep 2004	Larne	0	Ballymena United	1
Section C	18th Sep 2004	Lisburn Distillery	3	Institute	0
Section C	21st Sep 2004	Ballymena United	1	Lisburn Distillery	1
Section C	21st Sep 2004	Institute	4	Larne	1

Section C – Final Table

	P	W	D	L	F	A	Pts	GD
1. Lisburn Distillery (QF)	6	3	2	1	13	4	11	+9
2. Ballymena United (QF)	6	2	3	1	9	7	9	+2
3. Institute	6	2	1	3	8	10	7	-2
4. Larne	6	2	0	4	5	14	6	-9

Section D	14th Aug 2004	Newry City	4	Omagh Town	2
Section D	17th Aug 2004	Coleraine	0	Glentoran	3
Section D	21st Aug 2004	Glentoran	3	Newry City	2
Section D	21st Aug 2004	Omagh Town	0	Coleraine	3
Section D	28th Aug 2004	Newry City	3	Coleraine	1
Section D	31st Aug 2004	Glentoran	4	Omagh Town	0
Section D	11th Sep 2004	Coleraine	1	Newry City	0
Section D	11th Sep 2004	Omagh Town	2	Glentoran	5
Section D	18th Sep 2004	Coleraine	2	Omagh Town	0
Section D	18th Sep 2004	Newry City	0	Glentoran	4
Section D	21st Sep 2004	Glentoran	1	Coleraine	1
Section D	21st Sep 2004	Omagh Town	1	Newry City	3

Section D – Final Table

	P	W	D	L	F	A	Pts	GD
1. Glentoran (QF)	6	5	1	0	20	5	16	+15
2. Coleraine (QF)	6	3	1	2	8	7	10	+1
3. Newry City	6	3	0	3	12	12	9	0
4. Omagh Town	6	0	0	6	5	21	0	-16

Quarter-Final	28th Sep 2004	Cliftonville	2	Ards	1	(aet)
Quarter-Final	28th Sep 2004	Glentoran	1	Ballymena United	0	
Quarter-Final	28th Sep 2004	Linfield	3	Dunagnnon Swifts	1	
Quarter-Final	28th Sep 2004	Lisburn Distillery	1	Coleraine	0	

Semi-Final	19th Oct 2004	Cliftonville	1	Linfield	2	(aet)
		(played at the The Oval, Belfast)				
Semi-Final	20th Oct 2004	Glentoran	2	Lisburn Distillery	0	
		(played at Windsor Park, Belfast)				

FINAL – At Windsor Park – Attendance 6,000

9th Nov 2004	Linfield	1	Glentoran	2	(aet)
	Scorer: Picking (65)		Scorers: Lockhart (45), Leeman (63)		

Linfield: Mannus, McShane, O'Kane (Crawford 90), Hunter, Gault, Thompson, Simpson (King 46), Larmour, (D) Murphy (Picking 62), Bailie.

Glentoran: Morris, Nixon, Glendinning, Melaugh, Leeman, Holmes, Kilmartin (McCann 91), Keegan (McLaughlin 77), Morgan (McGibbon 108), Halliday, Lockhart.

Referee: D. Malcolm (Bangor)

Setanta Cup 2005

Group One	15th Mar 2005	Glentoran	2	Longford Town	1
Group One	4th Apr 2005	Longford Town	2	Linfield	1
Group One	19th Apr 2005	Linfield	3	Glentoran	2
Group One	25th Apr 2005	Longford Town	1	Glentoran	0
Group One	10th May 2005	Linfield	1	Longford Town	0
Group One	17th May 2005	Glentoran	2	Linfield	4

Group One – Final Table

	P	W	D	L	F	A	Pts	GD
1. Linfield	4	3	0	1	9	6	9	+3
2. Longford Town	4	2	0	2	4	4	6	-
3. Glentoran	4	1	0	3	6	9	3	-3

Group Two	22nd Mar 2005	Shelbourne	3	Portadown	3
Group Two	28th Mar 2005	Cork City	1	Shelbourne	0
Group Two	11th Apr 2005	Portadown	1	Cork City	1
Group Two	25th Apr 2005	Portadown	0	Shelbourne	1
Group Two	2nd May 2005	Shelbourne	1	Cork City	0
Group Two	16th May 2005	Cork City	0	Portadown	1

Group Two – Final Table

	P	W	D	L	F	A	Pts	GD
1. Shelbourne	4	2	1	1	5	4	7	+1
2. Portadown	4	1	2	1	5	5	5	-
3. Cork City	4	1	1	2	2	3	4	-1

FINAL – At Tolka Park, Dublin

| | 21st May 2005 | Shelbourne | 0 | Linfield | 2 |

Scorers: Ferguson (27), Thompson (37)

Shelbourne: Williams, Brennan (Moore 58), Hawkins, Rogers, Crawley, Baker (Ryan 25), S Byrne, Crawford (Ndo 58), Cahill, Hoolahan, J Byrne.

Linfield: Mannus, Douglas, OíKane, Gault, (W) Murphy, (D) Murphy, Thompson (Larmour 77), Mouncey (McCann 73), Ferguson, McAreavey, Bailie.

Referee: M.Courtney (Dungannon)